SOLO Taxonomy in Mathematics

Strategies for thinking like a mathematician

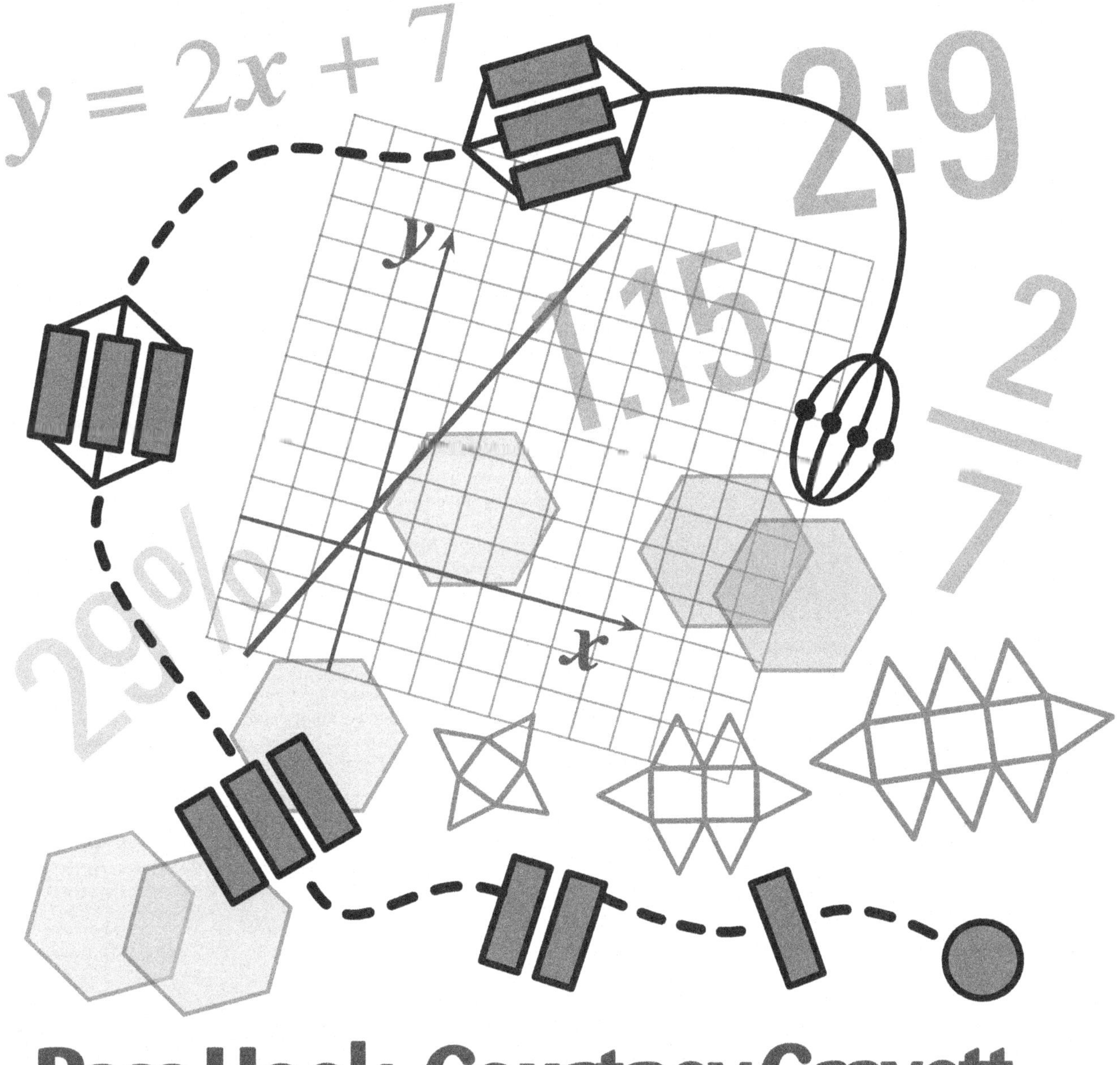

Pam Hook, Courtney Gravett, Mitchell Howard and Ellen John

Title:	SOLO Taxonomy in Mathematics Strategies for thinking like a mathematician
Authors:	Pam Hook, Courtney Gravett, Mitchell Howard and Ellen John
Editor:	Tanya Tremewan
Designer:	Diane Williams
Book code:	5861
ISBN:	978-1-77655-006-7
Published:	2014
Publisher:	Essential Resources Educational Publishers Limited

United Kingdom:	**Australia:**	**New Zealand:**
Units 8–10 Parkside	PO Box 906	PO Box 5036
Shortgate Lane	Strawberry Hills	Invercargill
Laughton BN8 6DG	NSW 2012	
ph: 0845 3636 147	ph: 1800 005 068	ph: 0800 087 376
fax: 0845 3636 148	fax: 1800 981 213	fax: 0800 937 825

Websites: www.essentialresourcesuk.com
www.essentialresources.com.au
www.essentialresources.co.nz

Copyright: Text: © Pam Hook, Courtney Gravett, Mitchell Howard and Ellen John, 2014
Edition and illustrations: © Essential Resources Educational Publishers Limited, 2014

About the authors: Pam Hook is an educational consultant (HookED Educational Consultancy), who works with New Zealand schools to develop curricula and pedagogies for learning to learn based on SOLO Taxonomy. She has published articles on thinking, learning, e-learning and gifted education, writes curriculum material for government and business, directs Ministry of Education e-learning contracts and is co-author of two science textbooks widely used in New Zealand secondary schools. She is known for her educational blog (http://artichoke.typepad.com) and is a popular keynote speaker at conferences.

Courtney Gravett earned a degree in mathematics at the University of California, Santa Cruz, USA and a Graduate Diploma of Teaching and Learning at the University of Canterbury, New Zealand. She has presented on her experiences of using SOLO in the mathematics classroom at the International Conference on Thinking and at the New Zealand Association of Mathematics Teachers Conference. Courtney was on the mathematics faculty at Lincoln High School for six years before becoming Assistant Head of Department Mathematics at Riccarton High School in Christchurch, New Zealand. She serves as an executive member of the Canterbury Mathematical Association.

Mitchell Howard has taught mathematics in Australia, the United Kingdom and New Zealand over the past 19 years. He completed an MEd (Mathematics) at the University of Canberra, Australia in 2005 and is currently the Head of the Mathematics Department at Lincoln High School and Vice President of the Canterbury Mathematics Association. He has also presented workshops at the New Zealand Association of Mathematics Teachers Conference, Mathematical Association of Victoria Conference and International Conference on Thinking. Mitchell is the proud father of two boys and is grateful for the support of his wife.

Ellen John has taught mathematics in the United Kingdom and New Zealand over the past 10 years. She has been Deputy Head of Mathematics and a leading teacher across a number of schools, specialising in interactive classroom teaching styles. She believes excellent mathematical teaching methods help to motivate weaker students to achieve more. She has presented at the International Conference on Thinking and New Zealand Association of Mathematics Teachers Conference on using SOLO in the classroom.

Acknowledgements: Thanks to Professor John Biggs for his encouragement and ongoing critique of the classroom-based use of SOLO Taxonomy. We are also grateful to Lincoln High School, Christchurch, New Zealand for providing the examples of student learning outcomes used in this book.

Copyright notice:

Schools and teachers who buy this book have permission to reproduce it within their present school by photocopying, or if in digital format, by printing as well. Quantities should be reasonable for educational purposes in that school and may not be used for non-educational purposes nor supplied to anyone else. Copies made from this book, whether by photocopying or printing from a digital file, are to be included in the sampling surveys of Copyright Licensing Limited (New Zealand), Copyright Agency Limited (Australia) or Copyright Licensing Agency (United Kingdom).

For further information on your copyright obligations, visit: New Zealand: www.copyright.co.nz,
Australia: www.copyright.com.au, United Kingdom: www.cla.co.uk

Contents

Introduction	4
1. SOLO Taxonomy and its potential for mathematical thinking	**5**
What is SOLO Taxonomy?	5
Applying SOLO to mathematical contexts	6
SOLO and thinking mathematically	7
2. SOLO problem solving strategy	**9**
How do we take a SOLO approach to problem solving?	9
Student examples	10
Self assessment rubrics	11
Key benefits	12
3. Multiple representations	**13**
How is multiple representation used?	13
Student examples	17
Self assessment rubric	19
Key benefits	19
4. HookED SOLO Describe ++ map	**20**
How is the Describe ++ map used?	20
Student examples	26
Self assessment rubric	30
Key benefits	30
5. SOLO Hexagons	**31**
How are SOLO Hexagons used?	31
Student examples	42
Self assessment rubric	44
Key benefits	44
Conclusion	**45**
Further resources: A selection of SOLO self assessment rubrics	**46**
References and further reading	**58**
List of tables, figures, templates and rubrics	**59**

Introduction

 Teaching students to think mathematically involves teaching them to master basic and problem-solving skills and strategies and to then use these to solve problems and to make meaning in familiar and unfamiliar contexts (Brosnan, Schmidlin and Grant 2013).

Various constructs have been used to distinguish between different levels of understanding when thinking mathematically. In New Zealand, the NCEA[1] standards for achievement, merit and excellence in mathematics and statistics are framed using the **multistructural**, **relational** and **extended abstract** levels of cognitive complexity in SOLO Taxonomy (Biggs and Collis 1982). Maths researchers like Chick (1998) have also used SOLO to classify different levels when students are thinking mathematically. Others have used terms like **instrumental and relational understanding** (Pesek and Kirschner 2000; Skemp 1976) or **procedural and conceptual knowledge** (Hiebert and Lefevre 1986).

It is important that educators continually evaluate the effect of their pedagogy when helping students think mathematically because research evidence suggests there are more and less effective approaches to teaching maths. We have found that using SOLO levels in the maths classroom has value because it enables students (and their teachers) to look at the quantity and quality of their own performance outcomes and make good decisions about their next steps. Explicit performance feedback, direct instruction, strategy-based teaching, challenge and mastery approaches have the most powerful effects on lifting student achievement outcomes in mathematics (Hattie 2009, p 145). Less effective are those approaches emphasising real-world applications, use of manipulatives, working within a peer group and using technology for independent practice (Hattie 2009, p 145). Some approaches – such as the use of calculators for basic operations with all real numbers, estimation and algebraic manipulation – can work against mathematical thinking (Ellington 2013).

Using SOLO as a lens through which to look at student outcomes helps maths educators and their students focus firmly on the complexity of the learning outcome, differentiating surface levels of understanding from deep and conceptual levels of understanding. As students move across the stages of the taxonomy, their mathematical thought increases:

- first in quantity, as students collect a growing number of loose mathematical ideas, information and facts (SOLO unistructural and multistructural levels)
- next in quality, as students relate and/or integrate these ideas (SOLO relational level)
- then conceptually, as students extend these related ideas to new contexts beyond the scope of the original problem or generalise them through the deduction of a general rule or proof (SOLO extended abstract level).

We believe that SOLO Taxonomy offers a powerful and efficient framework for students and teachers to represent the complexity of student mathematical understandings and explicit next steps and to prompt for these understandings. In this book, you can learn how to use the taxonomy to make learning outcomes visible in your mathematics classroom. We describe and explain different classroom-based SOLO strategies that provide a language and a vocabulary for explicit mathematical performance feedback by teachers to students, students to teachers, and students to students. Other useful SOLO strategies (for example, SOLO stations) are described in McNeill and Hook (2012, pp 6–11).

We note that all descriptions of how the strategies can be used (and student examples) come from the authors' experiences using SOLO with secondary maths departments in schools across New Zealand and especially in the Mathematics Department at Lincoln High School in Christchurch.

---

[1] The National Certificate of Educational Achievement (NCEA) is New Zealand's national qualification for senior secondary students. NCEA is part of the National Qualifications Framework.

1. SOLO Taxonomy and its potential for mathematical thinking

This section introduces SOLO Taxonomy and how it can contribute to mathematical thinking in the classroom.

What is SOLO Taxonomy?

 Structure of observed learning outcomes (SOLO) Taxonomy is a model of learning that describes student responses at five different levels of complexity – from prestructural, to unistructural, multistructural, relational and extended abstract (Biggs and Collis 1982).[1]

Figure 1.1: SOLO symbols and hand signs

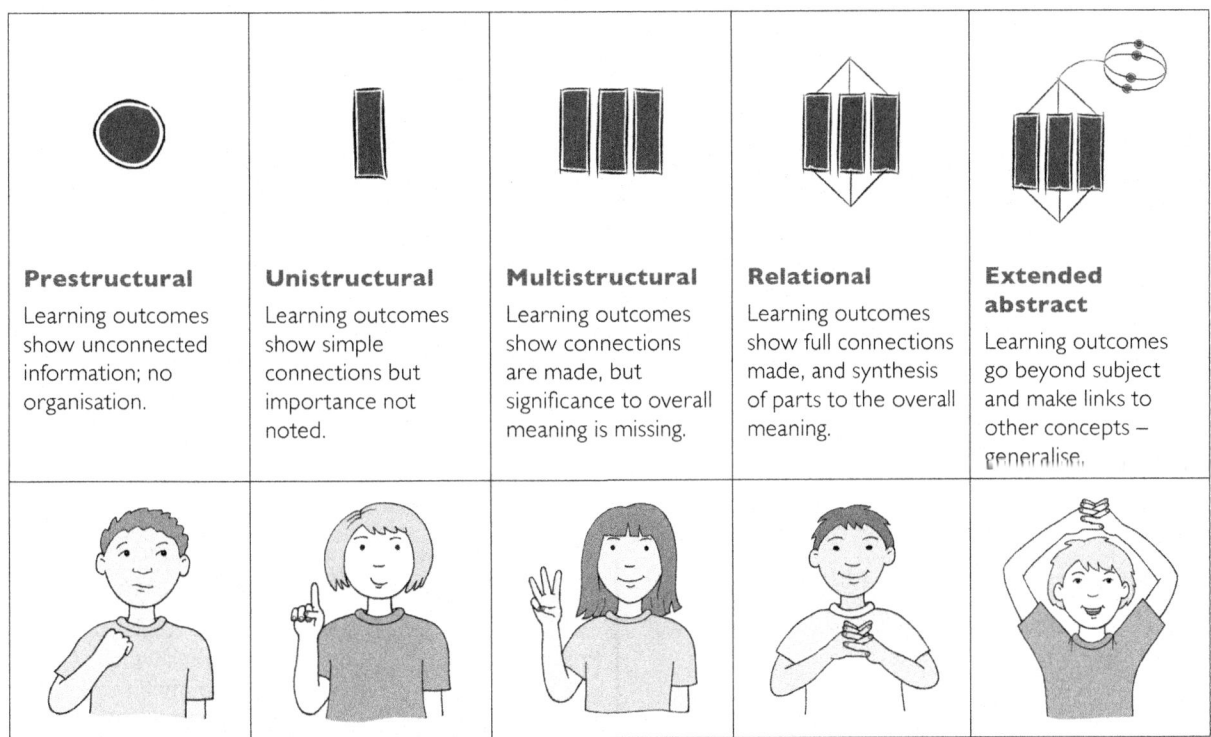

At the **prestructural** level of understanding, the task is inappropriately attacked, and the student has missed the point or needs help to start.

The next two levels are associated with surface levels of understanding – bringing in information. At the **unistructural** level, one aspect of the task is picked up, and student understanding is disconnected and limited. The jump to the next level is quantitative. At the **multistructural** level, several aspects of the task are known but their relationships to each other and the whole are missed.

The progression to relational and extended abstract outcomes is qualitative. At the **relational** level, the aspects of the task are linked and integrated, and contribute to a deeper level of understanding – and more coherent understanding of the whole. At the **extended abstract** level, the new understanding at the relational level is re-thought at another conceptual level, looked at in a new way, and used as the basis for prediction, generalisation, reflection, or creation of new understanding (Hook and Mills 2011).

In 2013 Professor John Hattie described SOLO Taxonomy as "the most powerful model for understanding these levels and integrating them into learning intentions and success criteria".

---

[1] For the story of how SOLO was developed, see Biggs (2013).

Applying SOLO to mathematical contexts

In a mathematical context, student responses at each SOLO level can be categorised in this way:
- **SOLO unistructural and multistructural** – one or many loose ideas, for example, using rules without reasons or knowing why it works, rote learning (surface understanding)
- **SOLO relational** – related ideas, for example, using rules with reasons, logical explanation and justification within the context of the problem (deep understanding)
- **SOLO extended abstract** – extending ideas, for example, where mathematical thinking is adapted and extended to make meaning of new situations that sit outside or beyond what is already known, and used to make generalisations (conceptual understanding).

Chick (1998, p 6) describes these levels from a mathematical researcher's perspective, progressing from: a prestructural understanding, in which the learner uses a data item incorrectly or simplistically; to unistructural, applying one concept or process, which will not necessarily lead to the correct conclusion; to multistructural, applying more than one concept or process but without synthesising them; to relational, synthesising processes, information and intermediate results and relating them to other information and processes; and ultimately to an extended abstract response, where the learner draws data or, more usually, concepts and processes "from outside the domain of knowledge and experience that is assumed in the question". Many other researchers have affirmed that SOLO's attributes of generality and objectiveness are valuable in maths education (Davey and Pegg 1989; Lake 1999; Moritz and Watson 1998; Van Rossum and Shenk 1984).

Also of note is that the task and the outcome can be at different levels of SOLO. For example, a unistructural task like "What is an acute angle?" can be answered at a prestructural, unistructural, multistructural, relational or extended abstract level. This can be seen in the HOT and HookED SOLO self assessment rubrics that support the HOT and HookED SOLO mapping (Hook and Mills 2011) but it is also evident when a SOLO relational response in one mode (developmental stage) of mathematical thinking becomes a unistructural response in the next cycle of unistructural, multistructural and relational understanding. As a consequence, there is no "race to the top". Indeed Chick (1998 p21) suggests that "if there is an upper bound on the number of cycles then it could be quite large. It is also conceivable that very few mathematicians will approach it".

Table 1.1 shows how UK maths teacher Gareth Williams has represented this "zooming in and out" facility in relation to fractions.

Table 1.1: Zooming in and out of fractions

Introducing fractions	Zoom in	Algebraic fractions	Zoom out
Prestructural	What is a fraction?	Prestructural	I am confident with fraction rules but have not tried them with algebra yet.
Unistructural	I can recognise a fraction.	Unistructural	I can simplify linear expressions with a denominator.
Multistructural	I can recognise a fraction. I can find equivalent fractions. I can simplify fractions. I can convert between fractions and mixed numbers. I can multiply integers.	Multistructural	I can simplify linear and quadratic expressions with denominators I can solve a linear equation with a denominator I can multiply algebraic fractions.
Relational	I can multiply fractions together and know how to deal with mixed number answers.	Relational	I can solve equations where algebraic fractions need to be multiplied.
Extended abstract	I can recognise when I need to use multiplying fractions in word problems. I am able to apply it to algebra.	Extended abstract	I can recognise when I need to do this in word problems. I can see how to use other fraction rules in the same way.

Source: Gareth Williams, willmaths, http://willmaths.wordpress.com/2013/02/24/zooming-in-and-out-of-maths-with-solo; used with permission of the author.

SOLO and thinking mathematically

In exploring how students think mathematically, academics and researchers have used SOLO levels to differentiate the structure of student learning outcomes in number and algebra, geometry and measurement, and statistics.

In the classroom, students use SOLO levels to look at their own achievement outcomes when using explicit and implicit cues to solve problems (see Table 1.2). Maths teachers use SOLO-coded questions as strategies to prompt students to deepen their understanding, move from one SOLO level to the next and reflect on their next steps (see Table 1.3).

Given that the task and outcome can be at different levels of SOLO, maths teachers and their students can make the complexity of the learning explicit in terms of both learning intentions and learning outcomes. This covers:
- what the student is doing (the complexity of the task – SOLO level)
- how well it is going (differentiated success criteria – SOLO levels)
- next steps (increasing the complexity of the next step – SOLO level).

The levels are communicated through SOLO symbols, hand signs (Figure 1.2) and co-constructed self assessment rubrics (Table 1.2; see also Sections 2–5 and "Further resources"), orally and by using strategies such as those described in the following sections:
- SOLO problem solving strategy
- multiple representations
- HookED SOLO Describe ++ map
- SOLO Hexagons.

In these ways students access the explicit performance feedback associated with raising student outcomes (see above).

Table 1.2: Self assessment rubric when working mathematically

Prestructural	I struggle to make sense of all the information. I don't know how to start. I guess.
	My solution simply restates the problem.
Unistructural	I can find one piece of information or heuristic that seems familiar and work on that.
	My solution identifies one relevant piece of information and uses it to perform a calculation, measurement or drawing.
Multistructural	I can use more than one piece of information in the problem but I cannot work out how they all connect to form a workable solution to the whole problem.
	My solution identifies several relevant pieces of information and uses them to perform calculations, measurements or drawings without offering any justification for my actions.
Relational	I can integrate my different calculations, measurements or drawings to form a workable solution to the problem and give a logical explanation for each step.
	My solution identifies several relevant pieces of information and uses them to perform calculations, measurements or drawings. I provide justifications (diagrams and words) for my actions deduced from the nature of the problem.
Extended abstract	I can generalise the integrated solution, introduce new elements, modify the solution and apply the solution to novel situations.
	My solution extends these justifications, making generalisations, abstractions and exceptions to include/integrate other variables and contexts.

Table 1.3: Question prompts to deepen students' mathematical thinking

Prestructural Needs help to start	**To move student thinking to the next level, ask:** • What can you see? • Where have you seen something like this before? • Have you heard of this before? • What does this remind you of? • What is [...]? • Can you define [...]? • What might be related to this? • Can you identify one key fact/formula/term? • What extra information do you need before you can start? • What sort of problem is this? • What does your textbook say about this sort of problem? • Can you find a similar or related example in your exercise book?
Unistructural Idea	**To move student thinking to the next level, ask:** • How did you get that answer? • What did you do to get that answer? • How did you work that out? • What does that mean? • How did you calculate that? • Can you identify any key facts/formulas/terms?
Multistructural Ideas	**To move student thinking to the next level, ask:** • Can you make links between these to find an answer to a question? • Can you explain what you did at each step and why you did it? • Can you show your working? • Why did you do that? • Can you add words to show how and why you did that step? • What is similar or different about this step? • Can you elaborate? • How do these ideas relate to each other?
Relational Integrate ideas	**To move student thinking to the next level, ask:** • Can you develop a proof or a general rule? • Can you think of a situation where the solution may vary from what you have calculated? • What is a use for this in everyday life? • Can you offer an algebraic proof? • Where could you use this reasoning in the world outside the classroom? • What are the implications of this reasoning? • Can you think of a situation where this reasoning may not hold true or may be limited? • Can you think of a situation where this will not work?
Extended abstract Extend ideas	**To further extend student thinking, ask:** • What does this make you wonder? • How effective was the process you used? • What modifications would you make if you were asked to work on a similar problem? • What would you change? • Can you extend these ideas to someplace new? • Can you look at this in a new way? • What did you learn from this that will be useful in the future?

Figure 1.2: SOLO hand signs in use in a mathematics classroom

2. SOLO problem solving strategy

Strategies for problem solving have been doing the rounds since George Polya published *How to Solve It* in 1945. If they have SOLO Taxonomy as a common language of learning, schools can use rubrics and symbols to help students develop their confidence in solving problems.

For some students, the hardest thing to do when solving a problem is starting. Claiming "I don't get it" or "I don't know", they appear reluctant to have a go. As they see it, there is a lot of information and an answer is not immediately obvious. They focus on what they don't know rather than looking for what they might know. They do not realise that, when looking at a problem, everyone starts at a SOLO prestructural level.

A competent problem solver will generally start by identifying and unpacking key information in the question (unistructural and multistructural outcomes); they will make connections between various parts of the question and link the information to knowledge or skills they have to form a strategy to solve the problem (relational outcomes).

After finding an answer, the good problem solver will check that it makes sense based on all they have learnt from the information in the question and what they know of the world. They might also review the strategy they have used and perhaps refine and rewrite their solution for publication. Another way they might check their answer is to try to solve the problem in a different way (extended abstract outcomes).

How do we take a SOLO approach to problem solving?

We can use a SOLO-type approach with students who do not know where to start on a problem so that they progress to become competent problem solvers. The following interaction illustrates how a teacher can use this approach with a student who is unfamiliar with the strategy.

> Teacher: Hey, this question is blank.
>
> Student: I can't do it
>
> Teacher: Have you read the question?
>
> Student: Yes, but I don't get it. *[Actually sometimes the reason they have not been able to start is that they have not even read the question.]*
>
> Teacher: There must be at least one thing in there that you know. Forget the overall question for now. Find one word or phrase that you know. (Are there some words that you have never seen before? Could you look them up?)
>
> Student: *[Finds one thing.]*
>
> Teacher: Can you represent that a different way? Can you … draw a picture of it? … write it as a number sentence? … make a list or table? … write a simple example of it?
>
> Student: Sure.
>
> Teacher: Okay, is there something else you can find out? *[Encourages multistructural outcome.]*

Once the student has located or "unpacked" several pieces of information, the teacher encourages them to make connections between these pieces of information. This **relational** phase is characterised by identifying, combining and applying two or more pieces of the puzzle to make new information. The student may then find this information helps to solve the problem, to understand the context or, later, to check their answer is feasible, or may find it is not useful at all.

Next the teacher directs the student to identify what this question actually wants you to find out. In standard problems, this information is usually given in the last sentence. By making connections or relating pieces of information, the student may now find that the answer is quite trivial. If the answer is not clear, then the student will need to return to try to unpack and combine more information from the question.

When the student reaches an answer, it is good practice to evaluate it – which is an example of **extended abstract** thinking. Here they consider the context, whether the answer makes sense in the real world, and whether the units and rounding used are sensible (eg, is "0.0035 km" or "the jar contained 257.345 ml" appropriate?). They may realise the answer will only be correct for certain conditions, such as water boiling point at sea level. They may add qualifications such as, "In real life a car travelling around a rectangular grid of streets could not keep a constant speed because it would need to slow down to turn the corners".

Student examples

These student examples demonstrate how the SOLO approach to problem solving worked with a student's strategy to solve a factorgram problem (Figure 2.1) and a HOT SOLO Describe self assessment rubric (Figure 2.2) which the student completed for this task.

Figure 2.1: Student strategy for factorgram "Describe" problem

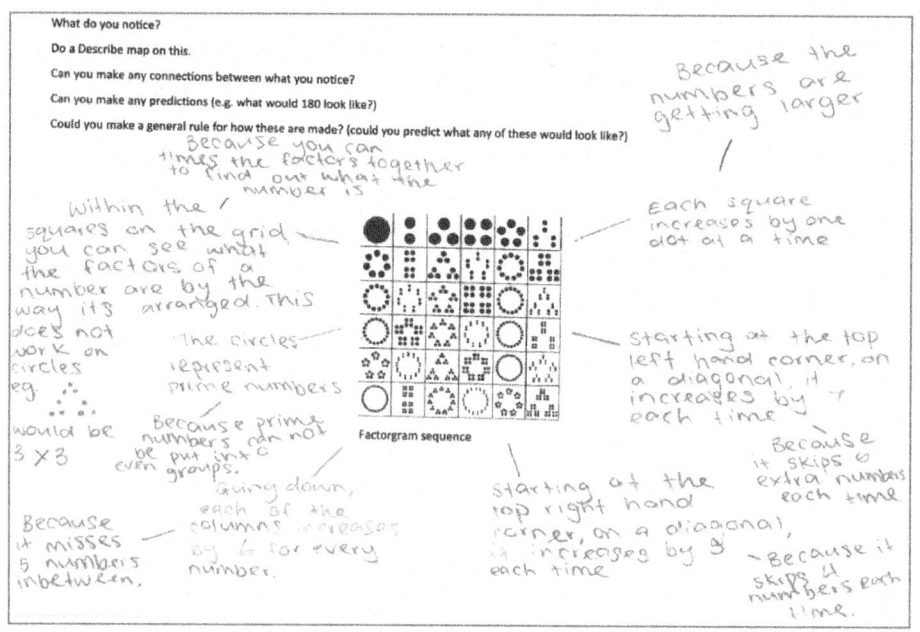

Figure 2.2: Student rubric for factorgram "Describe" problem

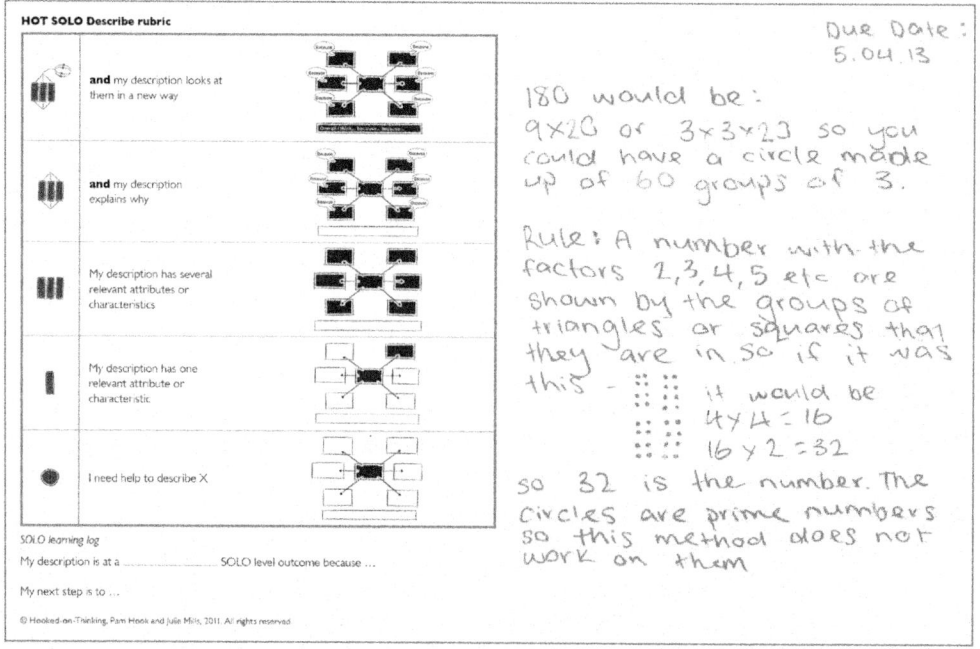

Self assessment rubrics

After attempting or solving a problem, a student could complete a SOLO self assessment rubric (with input from peers and the teacher) to identify where they think they are and see clearly what to do next. The following are examples of:

- a standard self assessment rubric (Template 2.1)
- a simplified version for less literate students (Template 2.2).

Template 2.1: Standard self assessment rubric for problem solving

SOLO level	SOLO explanation	Assessment		
		Student	Peer	Teacher
Prestructural	I have not started.			
Unistructural	I have found one thing in the question that I know. I can do something with this information such as write a number sentence, draw a picture, or make a table or graph. I might have made up an example for the situation with easy numbers or just written part of the question in a simpler way (summarised).			
Multistructural	I found other things in the question that I know. I have used these to write number sentences, draw pictures, etc.			
Relational	I have connected pieces of information from the question to learn more about the problem, or applied some other knowledge or skills to this information to learn more about the problem. By sorting and combining the pieces of information and learning more about the problem, I may develop a strategy that leads to a solution.			
Extended abstract	I have an answer to the problem and have checked that my answer makes sense and is communicated in a sensible way (using appropriate rounding and units). I have checked that someone else reading my solution would be able to follow my thinking and come to the same conclusion. I may have explained limitations of my answer by considering real world factors.			

© Essential Resources Educational Publishers Ltd

Template 2.2: Simplified self assessment rubric for problem solving

SOLO level	SOLO explanation	Assessment		
		Student	Peer	Teacher
Prestructural	I haven't started.			
Unistructural	Unpack one part.			
Multistructural	Unpack more parts.			
Relational	Make sense of the parts. How do they fit together?			
Extended abstract	Evaluate findings. Make sense of answers and method.			

Key benefits

Key benefits of using SOLO Taxonomy in solving problems are that this approach:
- promotes a "growth mindset" – an attitude that intelligence or talent is not fixed. Anyone is capable of developing their thinking and problem solving ability if they have determination and good strategies
- provides students with an easy way to start a problem, which some students find is the hardest part
- uses the common SOLO language of learning which students should be familiar with from their other learning areas
- differentiates work for students by indicating "where to next". All problems can be taken further and thought about at a deeper level. The SOLO framework provides cues to lead students to thinking more deeply.

3. Multiple representations

Ideas and concepts in mathematics can always be represented in more than one way. Students are often presented with these different representations in isolation and their connections are not made explicit. It is when a learner can make connections between these representations that they start to make sense of the bigger picture. As their understanding develops, they:
- become more flexible in their approach to solving problems
- find it easier to recall facts and processes and to check their solutions.

Diagrams, graphs, tables, metaphors, symbols, numbers, algebra, algorithms and matrices are examples of ways to communicate and understand processes or ideas in mathematics. Some ways make it easy for a person to see what is happening but take longer to do, such as using pictures to convert an "improper fraction" to a "mixed numeral". Others can be more algorithmic in nature, designed to reduce the cognitive load and speed up the process to arrive at a solution.

Unfortunately students in mathematics classes are often only shown the "quick way" which can lead them to think that "maths doesn't make sense to me so I must not have a 'maths brain'". Students become much more willing to use algorithms if the concept is introduced through the use of a longer way that "makes sense" and they are then offered an alternative. Some students might be happy to stay with the method that makes sense to them while others will be keen to move on to the "short cut" method. Either way the learning of mathematics should be presented as a sense-making exercise that can be done in more than one way.

As Malcolm Swan (2005, p9) advocates, we need to help move the perception of mathematics from being "a given body of knowledge and standard procedures that has to be covered" to that of "an interconnected body of ideas and reasoning processes".

How is multiple representation used?

Gaining an understanding of linear relationships is an important milestone in high school mathematics. The concepts can be presented as number patterns, tables of values, matchstick or dot patterns, taxi charge examples, equations and graphs on the Cartesian number plane. Students need to know how to do such things as plotting graphs, finding intercepts, using rates or gradients and making predictions. They often feel overwhelmed with all the material that they "have to remember". We need to give them the opportunity to see how these representations all fit together and that they are all just versions of the same thing. The big picture needs to be made explicit.

By Year 11 in New Zealand most students will have had some exposure to some of these concepts. We start work on *Investigate relationships between tables, equations and graphs* by discussing all the ways that number patterns can be represented and coming up with examples in each case (see Figure 3.1).

Students are then given the four scenarios to investigate as set out in Figures 3.2 to 3.5. The first two scenarios (Figures 3.2 and 3.3) are similar in that they start with a "matchstick pattern" but the others (Figures 3.4 and 3.5) have different starting points which allow students to be creative when designing the picture for the pattern.

This introduction to the topic:
- uses students' prior knowledge – they should also be encouraged to collaborate and compare their work
- gives the 'big picture' and sets the scene for future work on the individual components by providing a framework students can refer back to.

The same process can be repeated when it comes to looking at quadratic patterns (Figures 3.6 and 3.7).

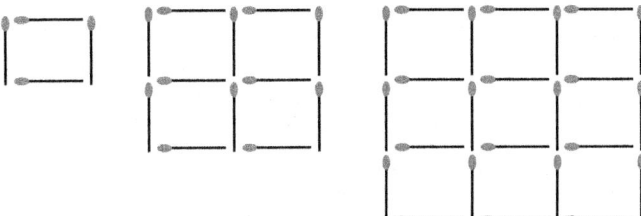

Figure 3.1: How can we represent number patterns?

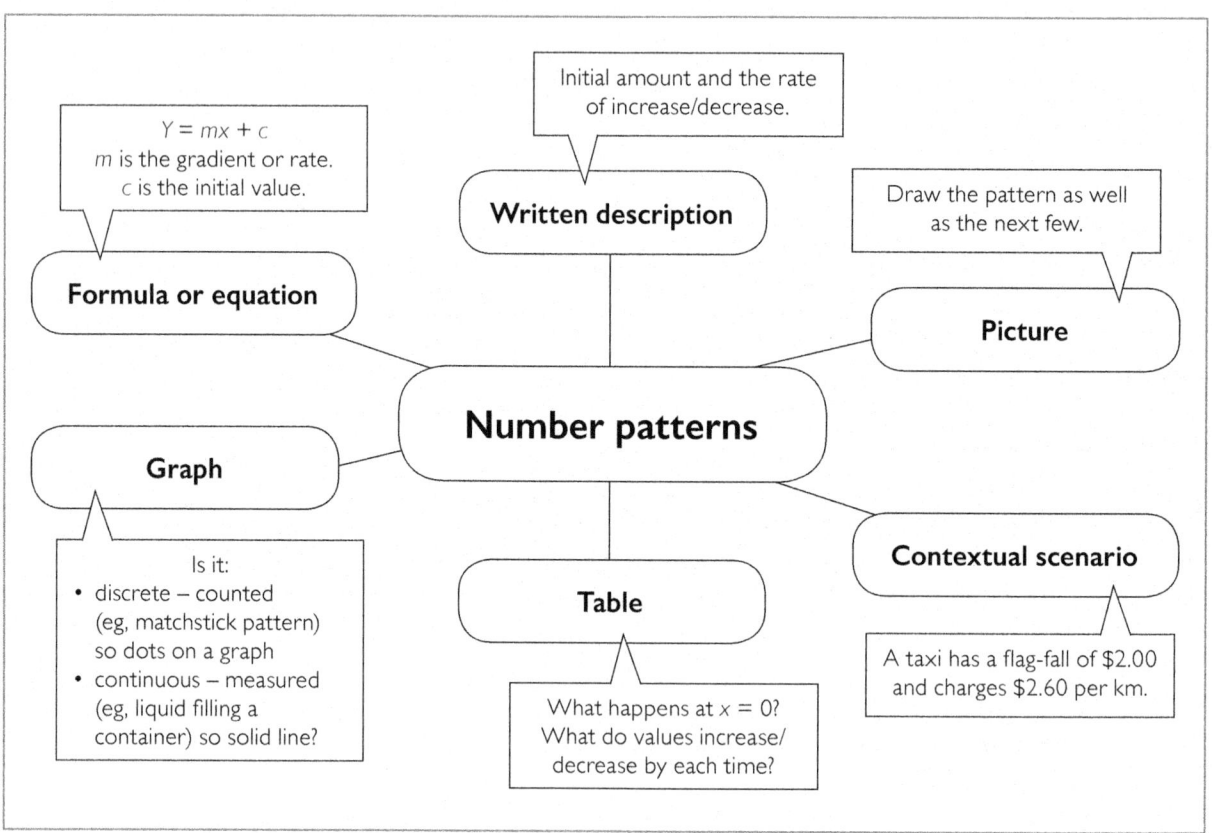

Figure 3.2: Linear pattern (a) – Building a fence

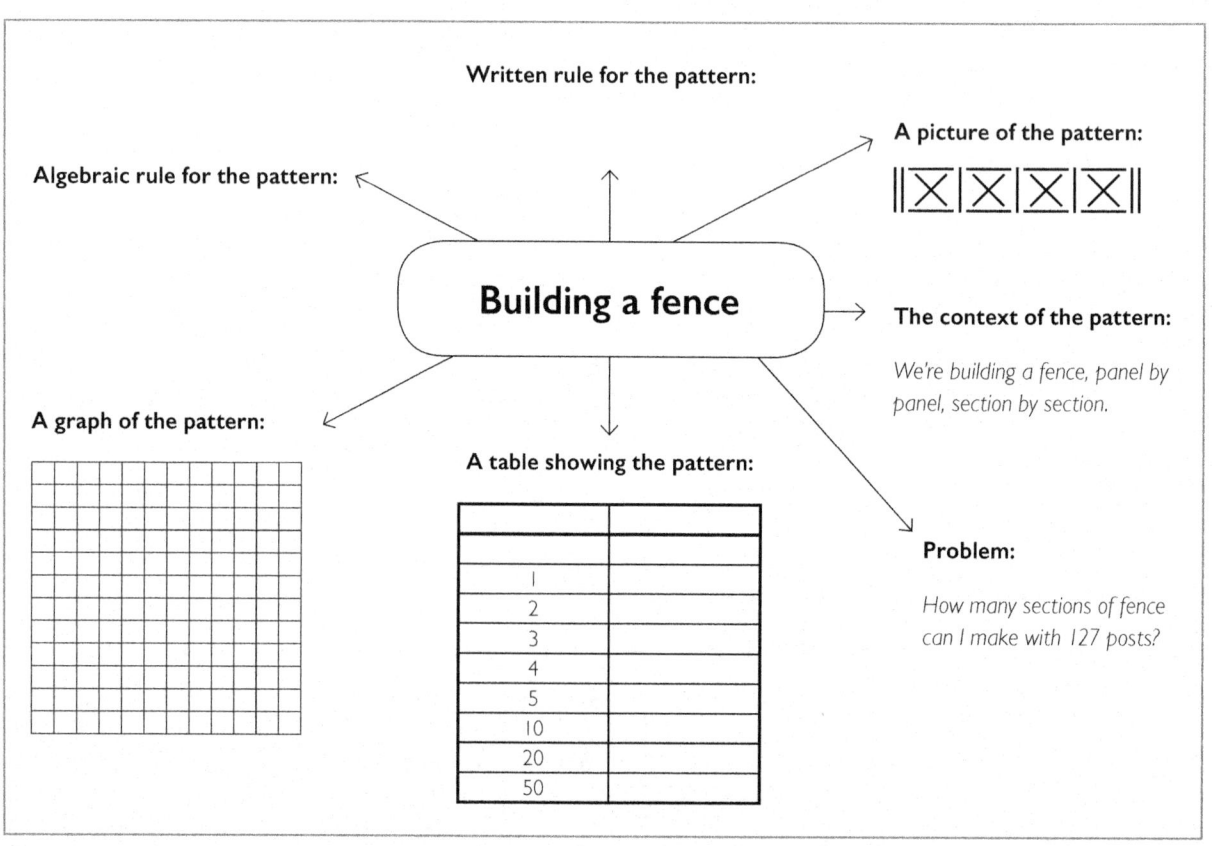

Figure 3.3: Linear pattern (b) – Matchstick pattern

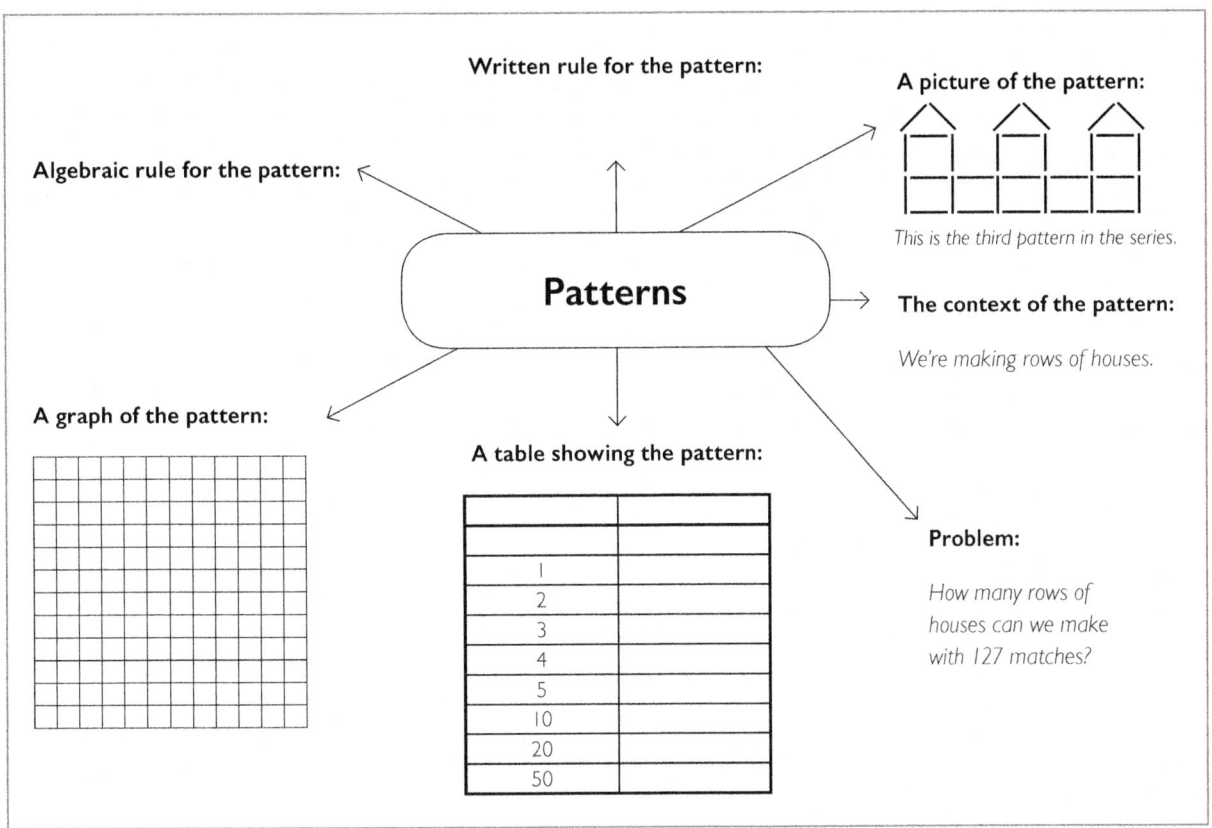

Figure 3.4: Linear pattern (c) – Taxi ride

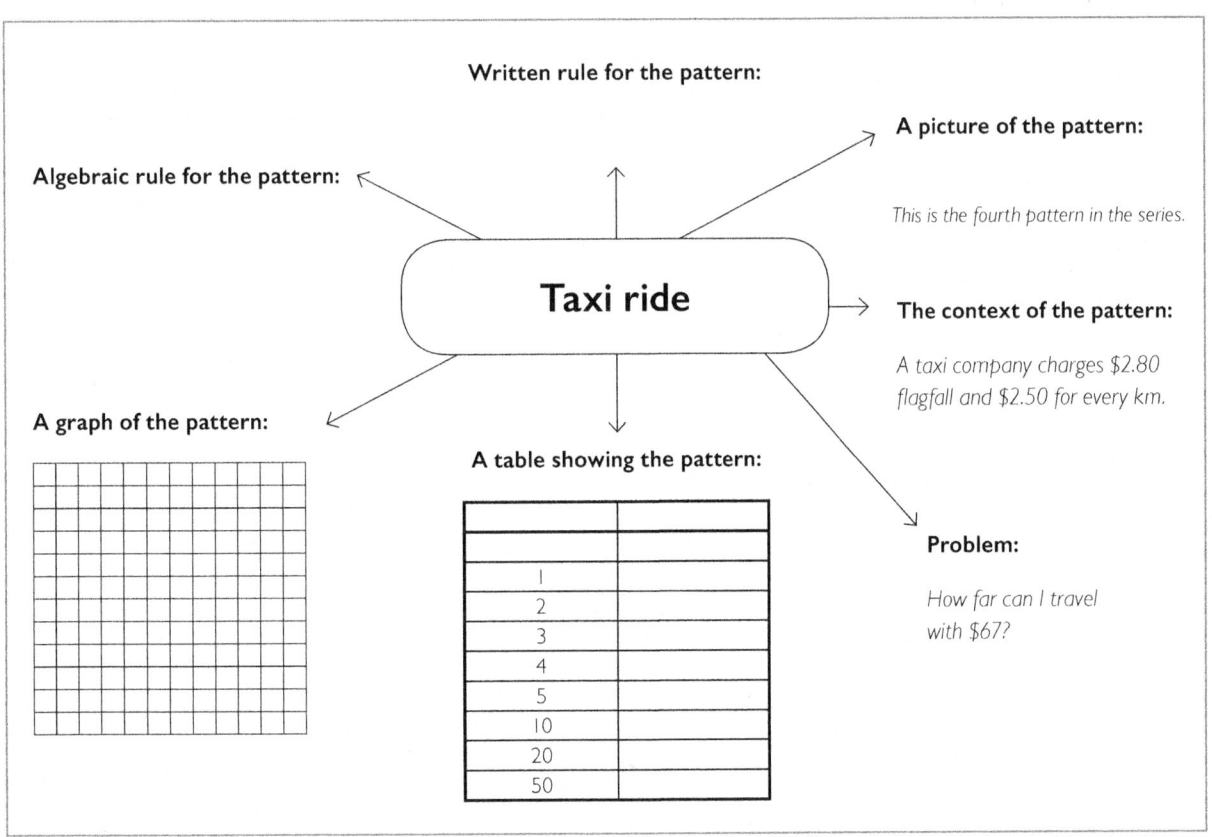

15

Figure 3.5: Linear pattern (d) – Make up your own

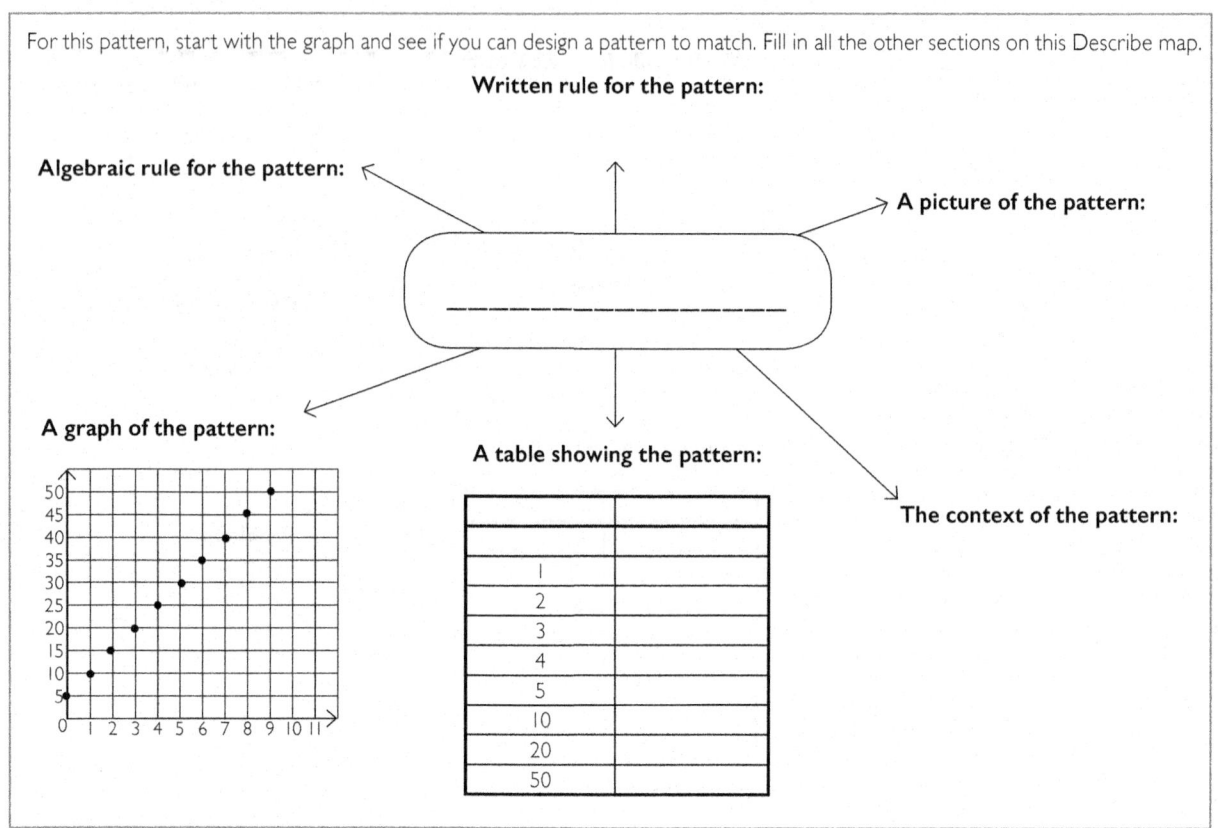

Figure 3.6: Quadratic pattern (a) – Matchsticks

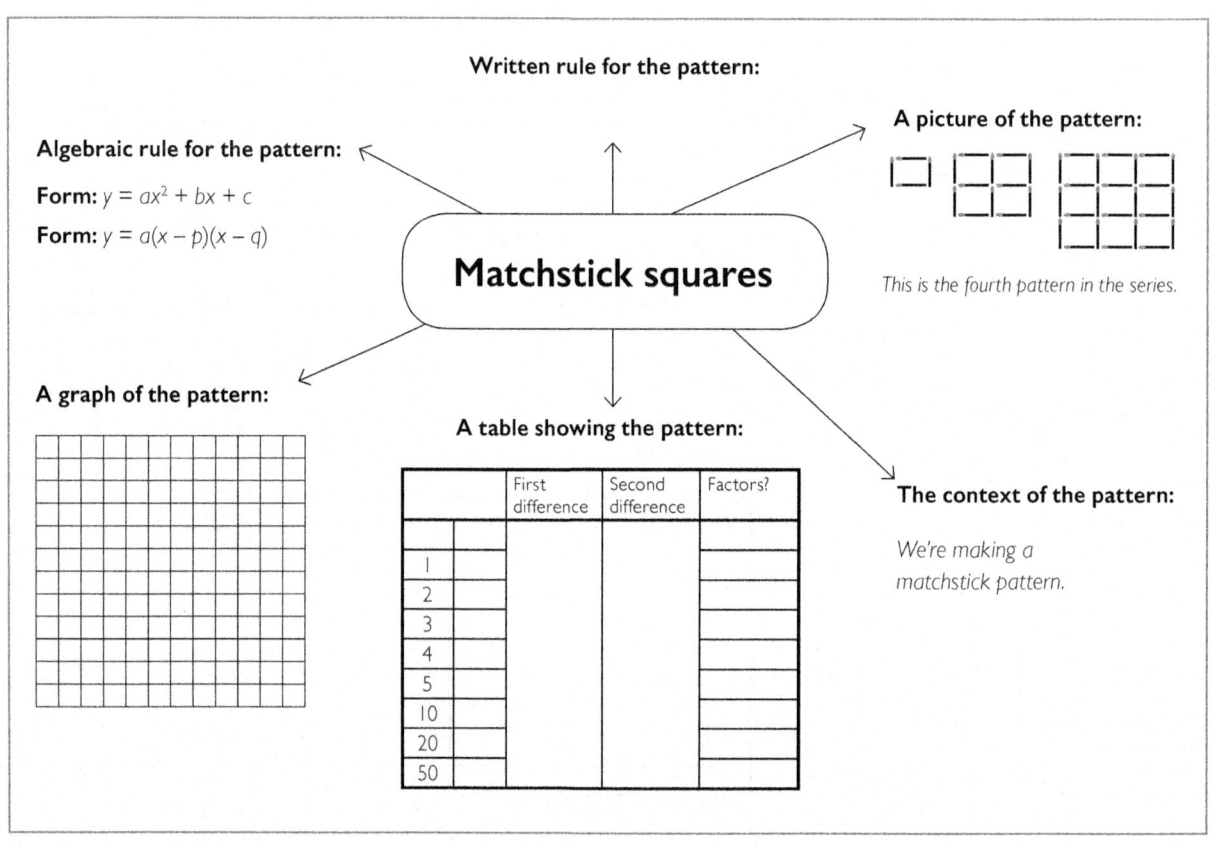

Figure 3.7: Quadratic pattern (b) – Handshakes

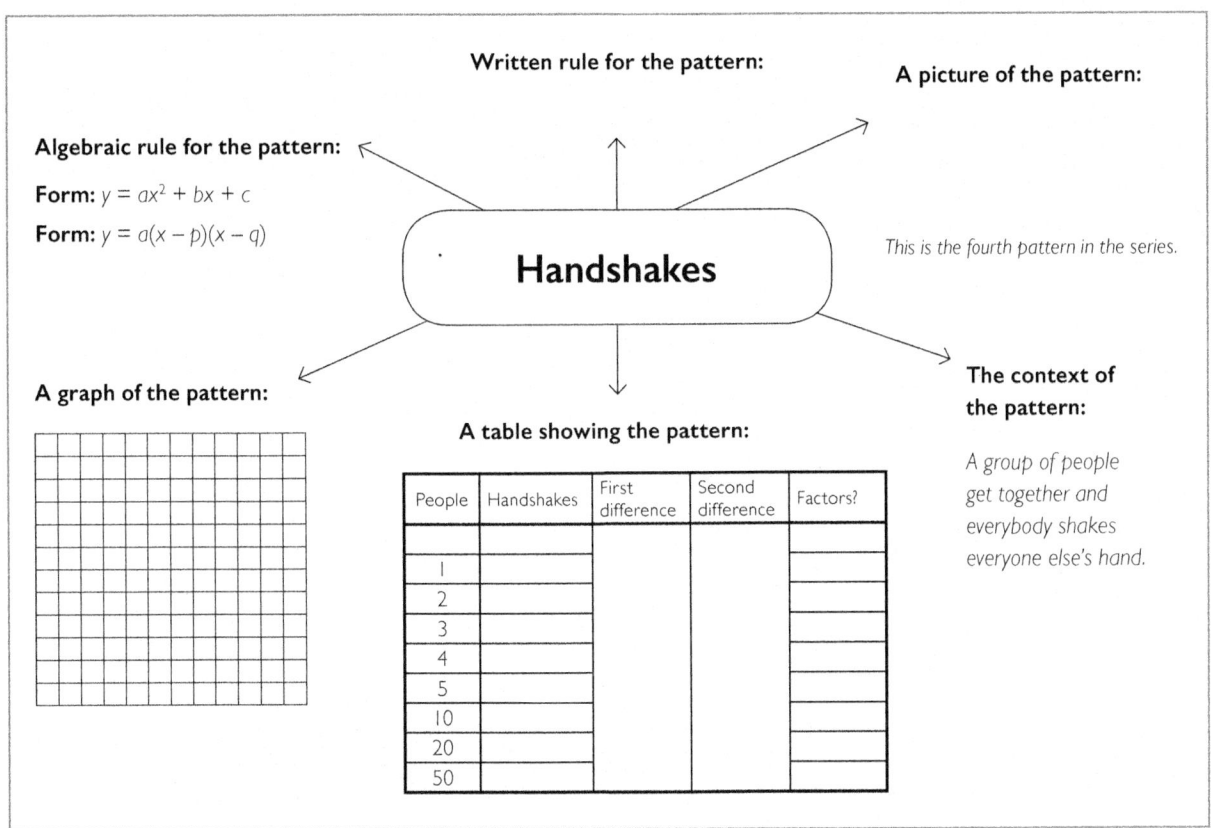

Student examples

Figure 3.8 presents a Year 9 student's work in creating and making links using like terms. Expectations about levels of thinking can differ according to the age group. In this activity, a student is showing:

 multistructural understanding by completing the table

 relational thinking by making connections to graphing and algebraic skills.

 extended abstract thinking by coming up with their own questions or investigations such as what would happen if there was a change in the initial conditions of the problem.

The next example (Figure 3.9) is from a Year 10 class assessment. Students demonstrate their relational thinking in this task by justifying their "rule" and by making sense of other students' answers (proofs).

Figure 3.8: Year 9 student creates and makes links using like terms

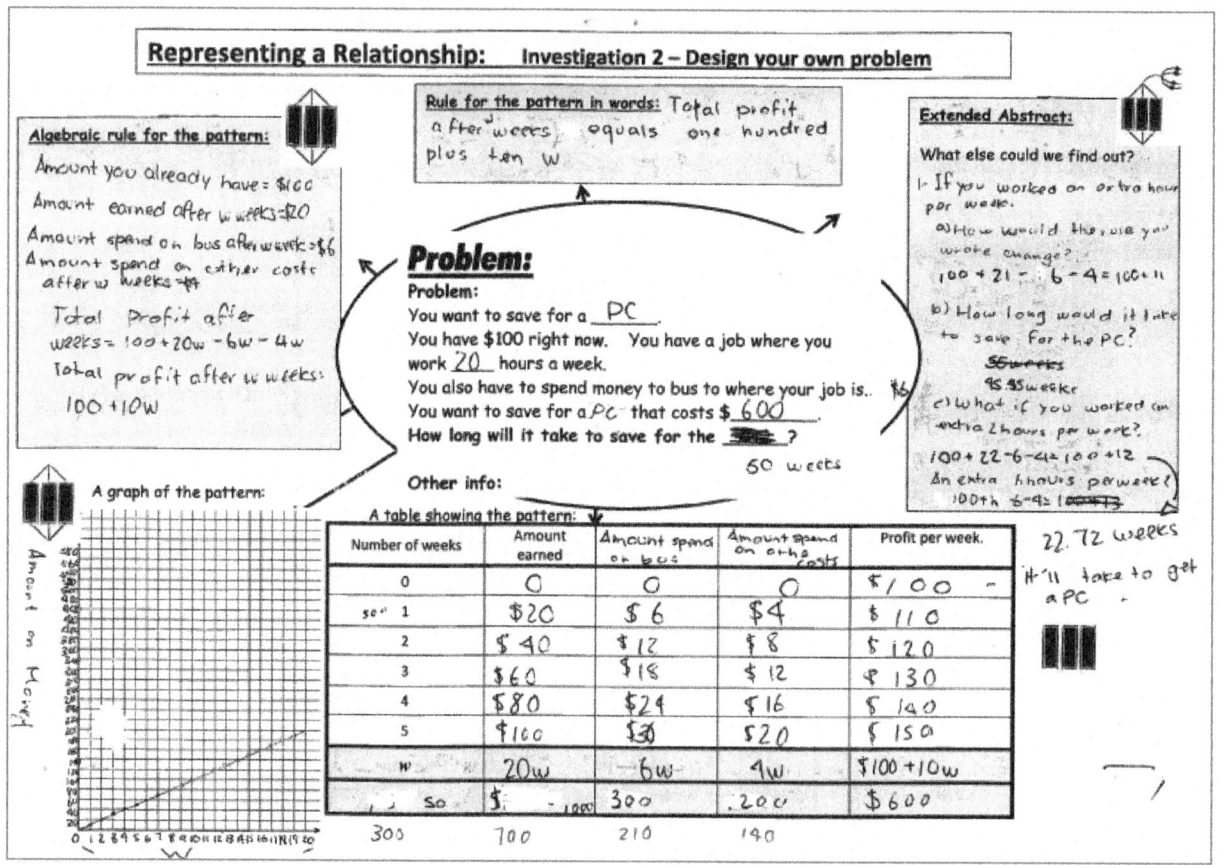

Figure 3.9: Year 10 student's response to a class assessment

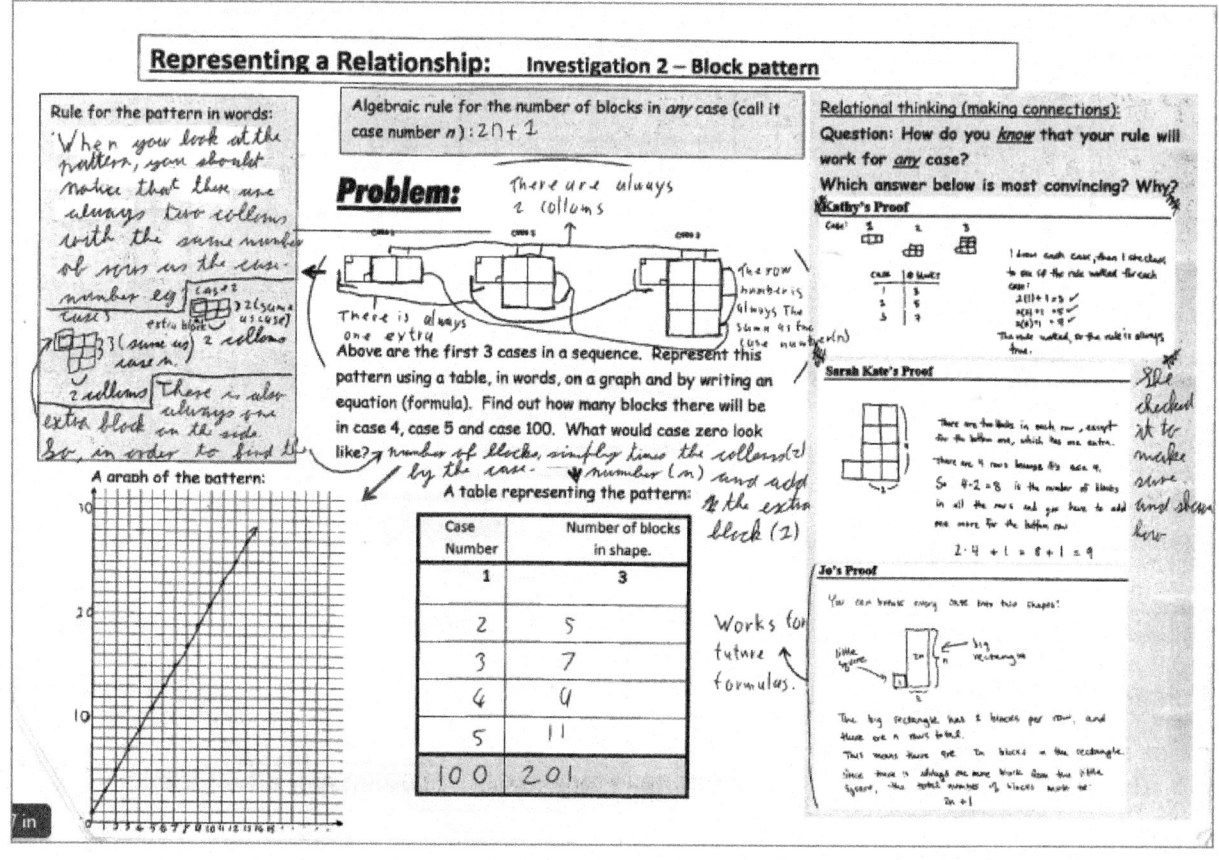

Self assessment rubric

Template 3.1: Self assessment rubric for representing number patterns

SOLO level	SOLO explanation	Assessment		
		Student	Peer	Teacher
Prestructural	I need help to get started.			
Unistructural	I can represent/interpret the pattern in one way.			
Multistructural	I can represent/interpret the pattern in more than one way.			
Relational	I am able to identify the features of linear patterns in the different representations. I can choose the best representation to solve a problem.			
Extended abstract	I can generalise a pattern and use it to solve a problem or make a prediction. I can evaluate the strengths and weaknesses of each of the representations.			

Key benefits

The following are some of the key benefits of using multiple representations for teaching mathematics:

- It gives students a view of the big picture, on which they can then hang other learning.
- It highlights the view of mathematics as an interconnected body of ideas and processes rather than a list of individual skills to cover. When students start to recognise the connections and similarities between the various components of this network of knowledge then mathematics becomes a lot less daunting. The learner views mathematics as a process of sense making rather than memorisation.
- It emphasises that there is more than one way to think about concepts and solve problems.

4. HookED SOLO Describe ++ map

The HookED Describe ++ map offers a useful strategy for helping students think mathematically. It scaffolds for surface, deep and conceptual learning outcomes when they are thinking like a mathematician, as well as providing prompts for oral and written language outcomes of simple sentences, complex sentences and mathematical statements.

The Describe ++ map prompts students to think at multistructural, relational and extended abstract levels. It helps maths students to plan learning outcomes for achievement, merit and excellence levels in NCEA.

Students (and teachers) can adopt a scaffolded approach by first using a partial map – the Describe + map (Template 4.1) – before moving on to the full Describe ++ map (Template 4.2).

Key

Note that in each template:

☐ small rectangles describe the key information

💬 speech bubbles explain what this information means when you think like a mathematician.

In the Describe ++ map, there are also thought bubbles that ask students to consider any variation in the possible answer – they prompt students to evaluate the context and/or validity of the answer, to extend the concept in another way or make a mathematical generalisation, or to deduce a general rule or mathematical proof.

How is the Describe ++ map used?

One way to use the Describe ++ map is to help students to break down large quantities of information into smaller and more manageable chunks.

For example, with the support of the HookED Describe ++ map students have been able to break down tasks when working at Level 1 with the NCEA numerical reasoning standard. The numerical reasoning standard has one long question rather than discrete skill-based questions. To answer this question successfully, students need to have the literacy skills of being able to:

- read the question
- identify key information
- use key information to solve problem
- structure their written answer.

Step 1: To help students develop these skills, we presented the information needed to solve the King Arthur's College problem in a Describe + map, but left out the overall question (Figure 4.1). We asked the students to work in groups to:

- identify the key information and place this in the rectangular boxes
- carry out a mathematical calculation based on the information and put this into the speech bubbles (Achieved level) (see Figure 4.3 in the student examples section for two students' responses).

Step 2: Still without knowing the question, the students were instructed to:

- identify what you can work out (calculate) from the information given
    For example, I can calculate the number of boys.
- calculate the answer to the questions
- complete the different sections of the sheet with your group – make sure everyone agrees with the answers.

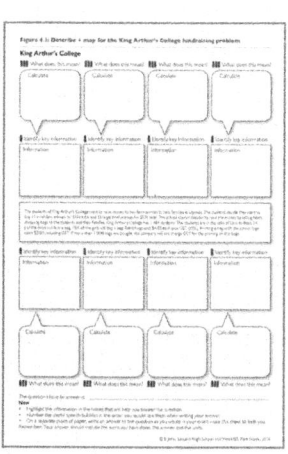

Template 4.1: HookED Describe + map

Title: _____

▌▌▌ What does this mean?	▌▌▌ What does this mean?	▌▌▌ What does this mean?	▌▌▌ What does this mean?
Calculate	Calculate	Calculate	Calculate

▌ Identify key information	▌ Identify key information	▌ Identify key information	▌ Identify key information
Information	Information	Information	Information

Question

▌ Identify key information	▌ Identify key information	▌ Identify key information	▌ Identify key information
Information	Information	Information	Information

Calculate	Calculate	Calculate	Calculate

▌▌▌ What does this mean?	▌▌▌ What does this mean?	▌▌▌ What does this mean?	▌▌▌ What does this mean?

The question I have to answer is: _____

Now
- Highlight the information in the boxes that will help you answer the question.
- Number the useful speech bubbles in the order you would use them when writing your answer.
- On a separate piece of paper, write an answer to the question as you would in your exam – use this sheet to help you.

© E John, Lincoln High School and HookED, Pam Hook, 2014

© Essential Resources Educational Publishers Ltd

Template 4.2: HookED Describe ++ map

Title: _____

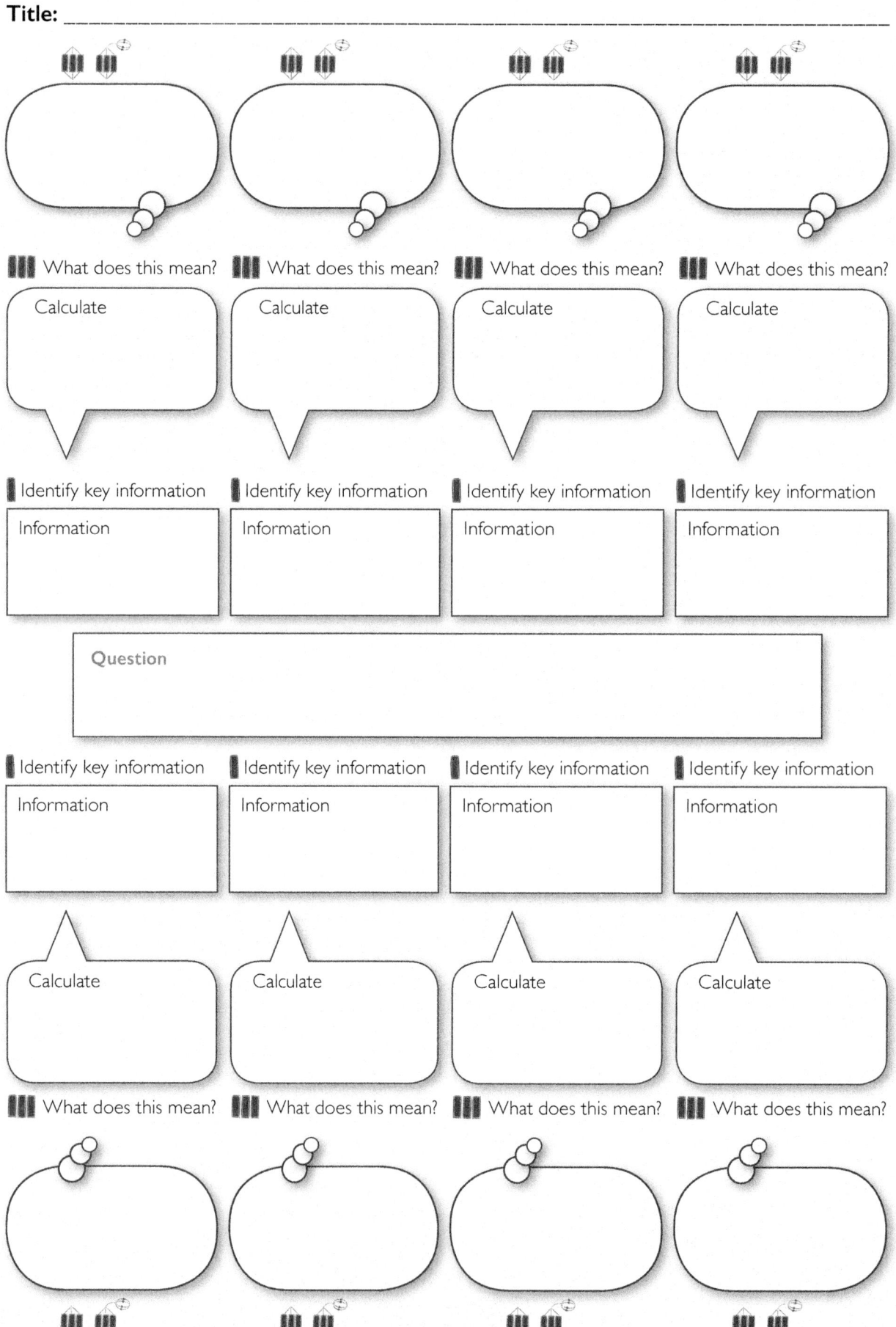

Figure 4.1: Describe + map for the King Arthur's College fundraising problem

King Arthur's College

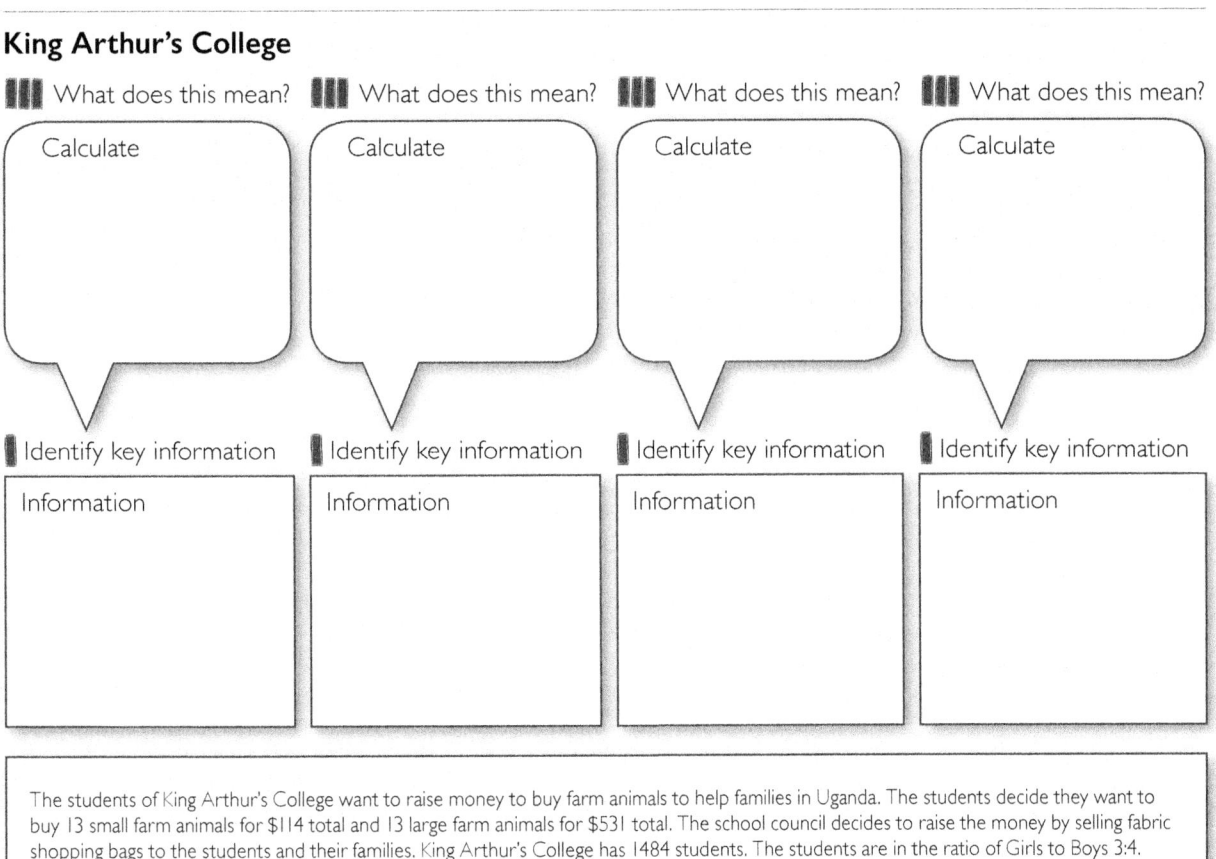

The students of King Arthur's College want to raise money to buy farm animals to help families in Uganda. The students decide they want to buy 13 small farm animals for $114 total and 13 large farm animals for $531 total. The school council decides to raise the money by selling fabric shopping bags to the students and their families. King Arthur's College has 1484 students. The students are in the ratio of Girls to Boys 3:4. $\frac{5}{8}$ of the boys will buy a bag. 75% of the girls will buy a bag. Blank bags cost $4.02 each plus GST (15%). Printing a bag with the school logo costs $3.00 including GST. If more than 1000 bags are bought, the company will not charge GST for the printing on the bags.

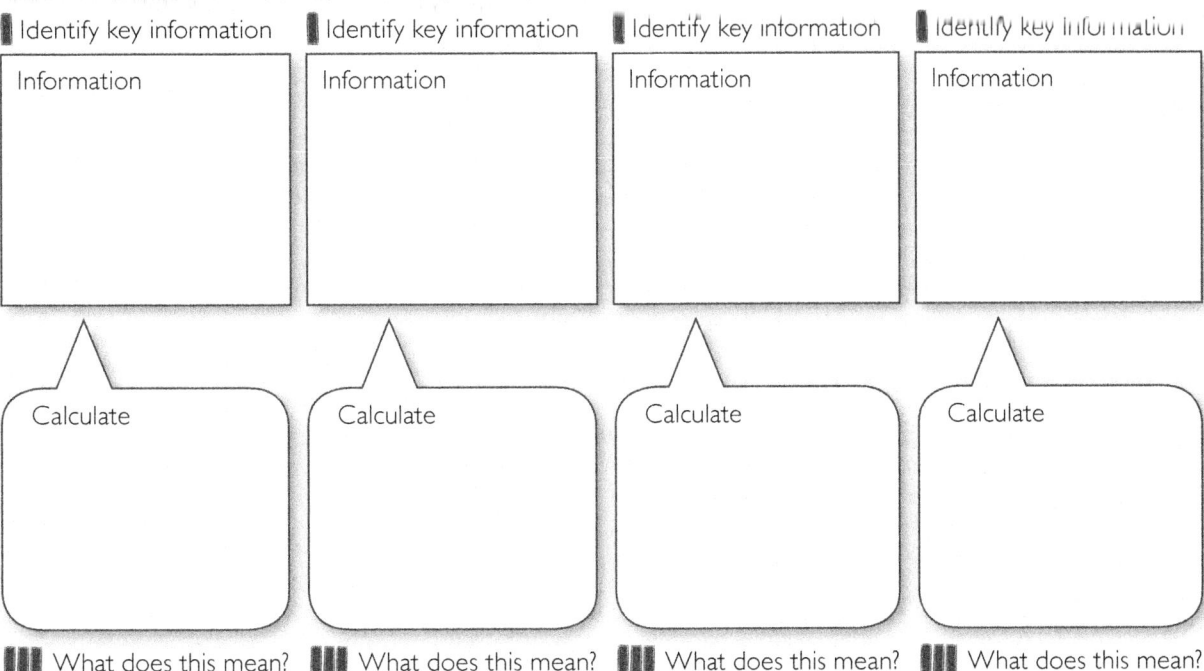

The question I have to answer is: _____

Now
- Highlight the information in the boxes that will help you answer the question.
- Number the useful speech bubbles in the order you would use them when writing your answer.
- On a separate piece of paper, write an answer to the question as you would in your exam – use this sheet to help you.
Remember: Your answer should include the sums you have done, the answer and the units.

© E John, Lincoln High School and HookED, Pam Hook, 2014

© Essential Resources Educational Publishers Ltd

23

Step 3: We gave the students the overall question for the problem: "What is the minimum price per fabric shopping bag you need to charge in order to raise enough money for the 26 animals?"

Their task was to structure an answer that included a written sentence for each mathematical statement in the speech bubbles on their Describe + map (Merit level).

Step 4: Students practised answering many questions of this type, using the Describe + map to help them structure each answer. The questions slowly became more complex, building up to examination standard.

Step 5: Once the students had become comfortable with the Describe + map, which is suitable for less involved questions, we moved on to the more complex Describe ++ map. Now students could include "What if" questions (Excellence level) with the outer layer of thought bubbles – such as in thinking about the variable exchange rate in the Mike and Huia question (Figure 4.2; for a sample of student responses, see Figure 4.4 in the student examples section).

Step 6: Once students were skilled at breaking down the longer questions, we extended their mathematical thinking by asking:

> What maths skills did you use to answer each of the questions?
> For example: I found a fraction of an amount.

The students' task was to write their own exam questions (which could then be used as other questions for practice). Their instructions were to work in pairs to:

- identify the skills being assessed in the Mike and Huia problem
- write a question to assess these same skills
- work out the answers to your question (you will be swapping questions, and then marking the answers from the people you swapped with)
- complete the self assessment column of the "Numerical reasoning – Writing the question assessment sheet" (Table 4.1).

Students filled out this assessment sheet because it:

- prompted them to think about the work that they had done and what they needed to do to improve on it
- aligns with the requirements of the numerical reasoning assessment (what is required at Achieved, Merit and Excellence levels).

Step 7: Each pair swapped their question with another pair's and attempted the other's question.

Step 8: Students filled out the peer assessment column of the other pair's assessment form. We directed them to frame their feedback positively, give explicit detailed descriptions to back up their claims and include feedforward suggestions for improving the question.

Step 9: Each pair returned their completed answer to the pair who created it. Each pair was to:

- mark the work by ticking or crossing the answers to say if the pair is correct
- give written feedback on how easy the answer is to understand, whether the working is clear and what the pair could do to improve their answer
- return the marked answer to the pair who did it so they can see how well they've done.

Step 10: Students sat a practice exam, which was marked by teachers on a separate marking scheme with no grade given on the students' papers.

Step 11: The students received their "ungraded" papers back, and used a student-friendly copy of the marking scheme to self-assess their papers. Students were encouraged to discuss their self assessment grade with their peers to see if they agreed. We then handed back the teacher-completed marking scheme. Students discussed, in groups and with the teacher, whether they agreed or identified any areas of contention.

Step 12: Students had an opportunity to add a sentence or paragraph to their answer to improve it. They also did several more practice exams in the lead-up to the real exam, where students used the Describe ++ map to help them to break down the question and organise the format of their response (see Figure 4.5 in the student examples section).

Figure 4.2: Describe ++ map for Mike and Huia's exchange rate problem

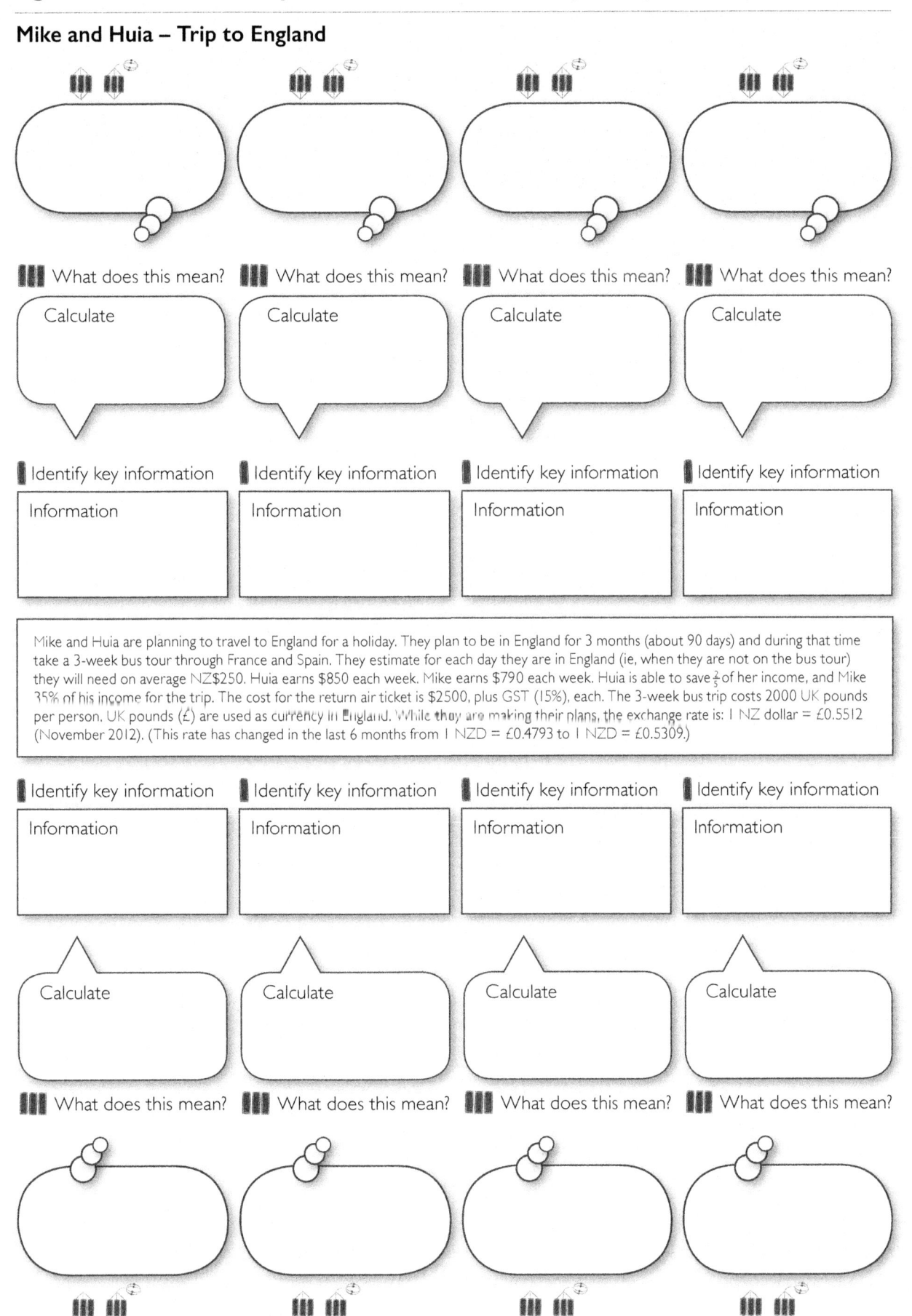

Mike and Huia – Trip to England

What does this mean? | What does this mean? | What does this mean? | What does this mean?

Calculate | Calculate | Calculate | Calculate

Identify key information | Identify key information | Identify key information | Identify key information

Information | Information | Information | Information

Mike and Huia are planning to travel to England for a holiday. They plan to be in England for 3 months (about 90 days) and during that time take a 3-week bus tour through France and Spain. They estimate for each day they are in England (ie, when they are not on the bus tour) they will need on average NZ$250. Huia earns $850 each week. Mike earns $790 each week. Huia is able to save $\frac{2}{7}$ of her income, and Mike 35% of his income for the trip. The cost for the return air ticket is $2500, plus GST (15%), each. The 3-week bus trip costs 2000 UK pounds per person. UK pounds (£) are used as currency in England. While they are making their plans, the exchange rate is: 1 NZ dollar = £0.5512 (November 2012). (This rate has changed in the last 6 months from 1 NZD = £0.4793 to 1 NZD = £0.5309.)

Identify key information | Identify key information | Identify key information | Identify key information

Information | Information | Information | Information

Calculate | Calculate | Calculate | Calculate

What does this mean? | What does this mean? | What does this mean? | What does this mean?

© E John, Lincoln High School and HookED, Pam Hook, 2014. Problem sourced from
http://ncea.tki.org.nz/Resources-for-aligned-standards/Mathematics-and-statistics/Level-1-Mathematics-and-statistics

© Essential Resources Educational Publishers Ltd

Table 4.1: Numerical reasoning – writing the question assessment sheet

SOLO level		SOLO explanation	Assessment		
			Student	Peer	Teacher
Prestructural		I needed teacher assistance to write most of the question			
Unistructural		My question only requires people to work out one answer. *For example: Find the price when GST is added to $50.*			
Multistructural		My question requires people to work out several different answers, but they don't link together. *For example: Find the price when GST is added to $50. Share $48 in the ratio of 1:2. Increase $45 by 15%.*			
Relational		My question requires people to work out several different answers that link together to give one overall answer. For example: *The students at King Arthur's College sponsor a child from Bangladesh. The cost of sponsorship is $1.50 per day or $547.50 a year. The 2011 School Council decides to raise the money by printing T-shirts and selling them to the students. King Arthur's College has 1260 students. The ratio of Boys to Girls is 5:4. 12% of the boys will buy a T-shirt. $\frac{2}{7}$ of the girls will buy a T-shirt. Blank T-shirts cost $8.50 each, plus GST (15%). Printing costs $1.20 per T-shirt including GST. If more than 200 T-shirts are ordered, the printing company will take off the GST. What is the minimum price per T-shirt that the School Council needs to charge in order to make the required $547.50 a year?*			
Extended abstract		My question involves some kind of variation that requires people to work out a range of different answers. This might be modelled or generalised through forming an equation. It may also involve some evaluation of the context or validity of the answer. *For example: You have the King Arthur's College question above, but you have to change the money into Taka (the currency of Bangladesh) and you have to allow for changes to the exchange rate.*			

Student examples

The following pages illustrate student responses to:
- King Arthur's College's fundraising problem, using the Describe + map (Figure 4.3)
- Mike and Huia's exchange rate problem, using the Describe ++ map (Figure 4.4)
- an exam question, supported by the Describe ++ map (Figure 4.5).

Figure 4.3: Student responses to the fundraising problem using the Describe + map

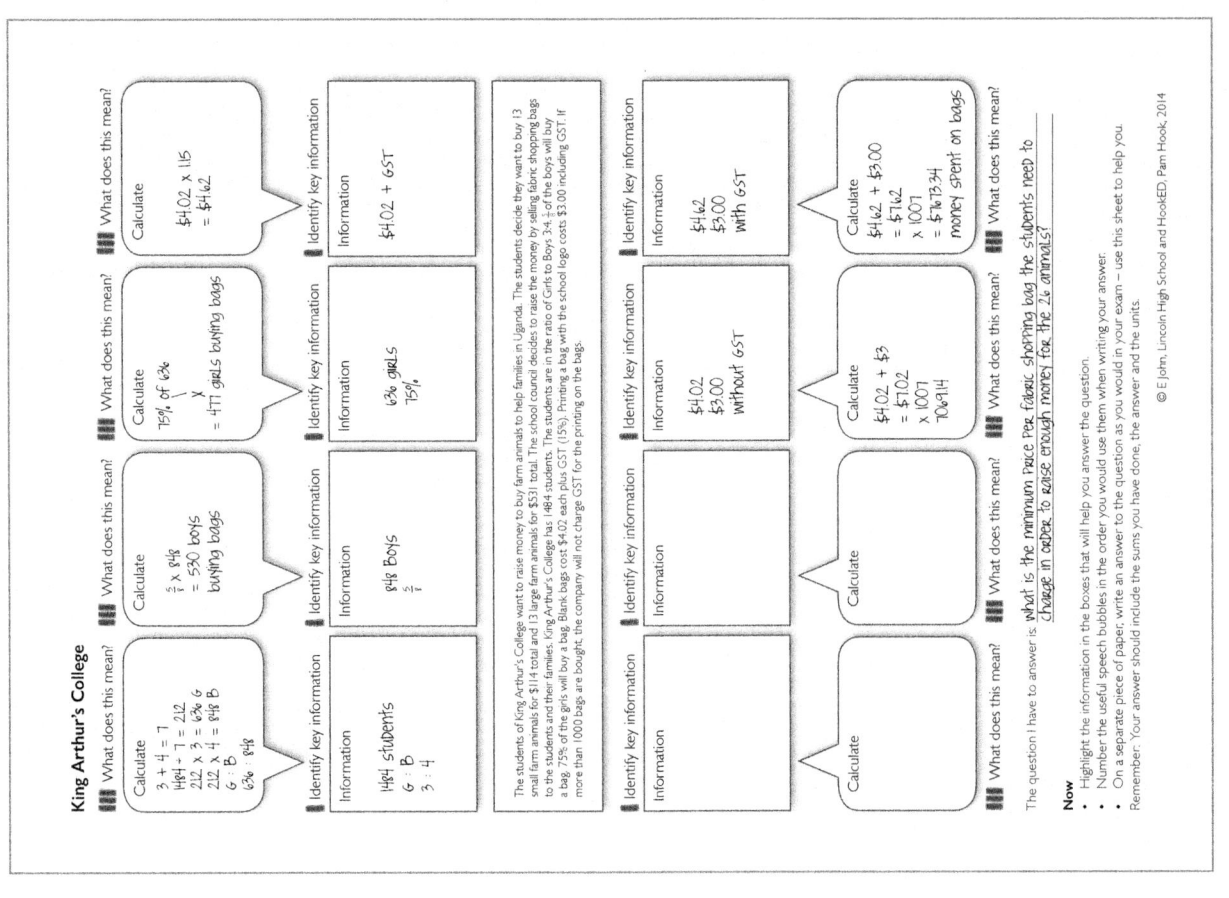

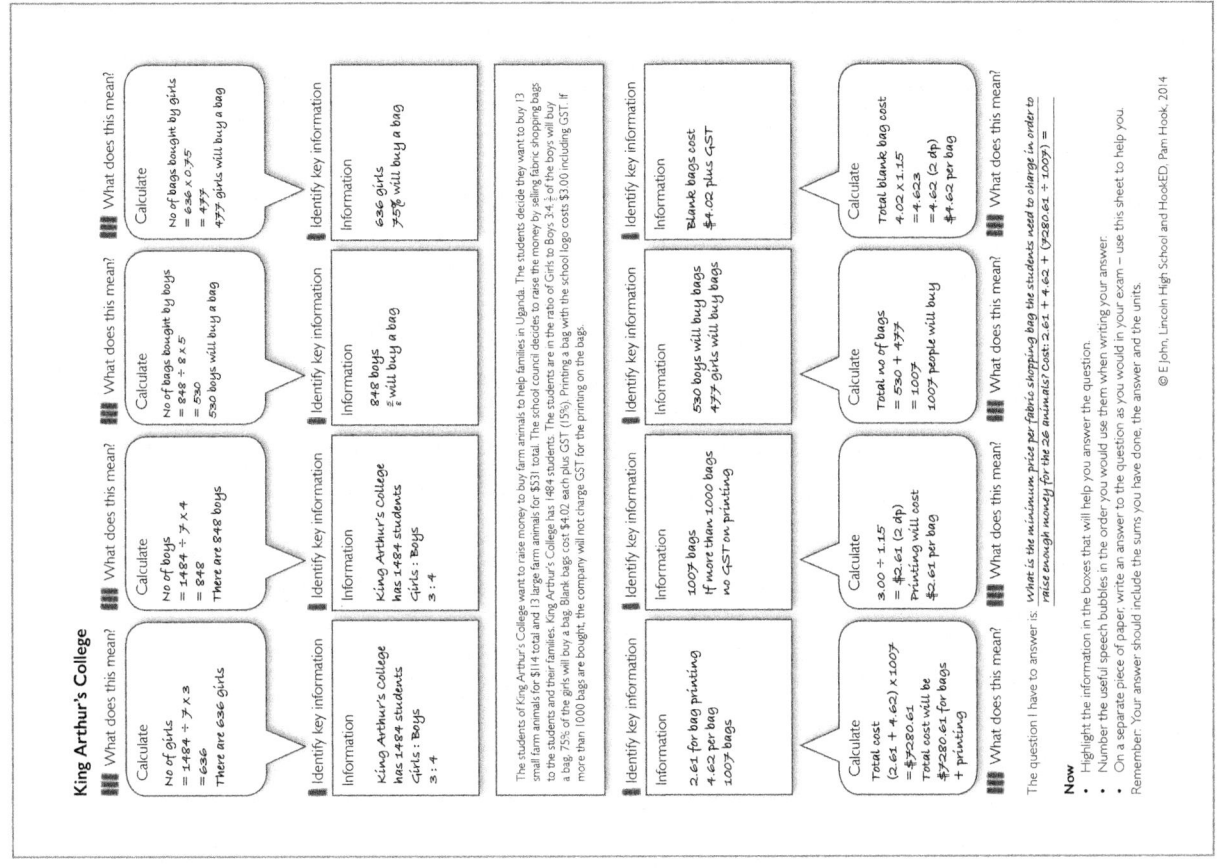

Figure 4.4: Student responses to the exchange rate problem using the Describe ++ map

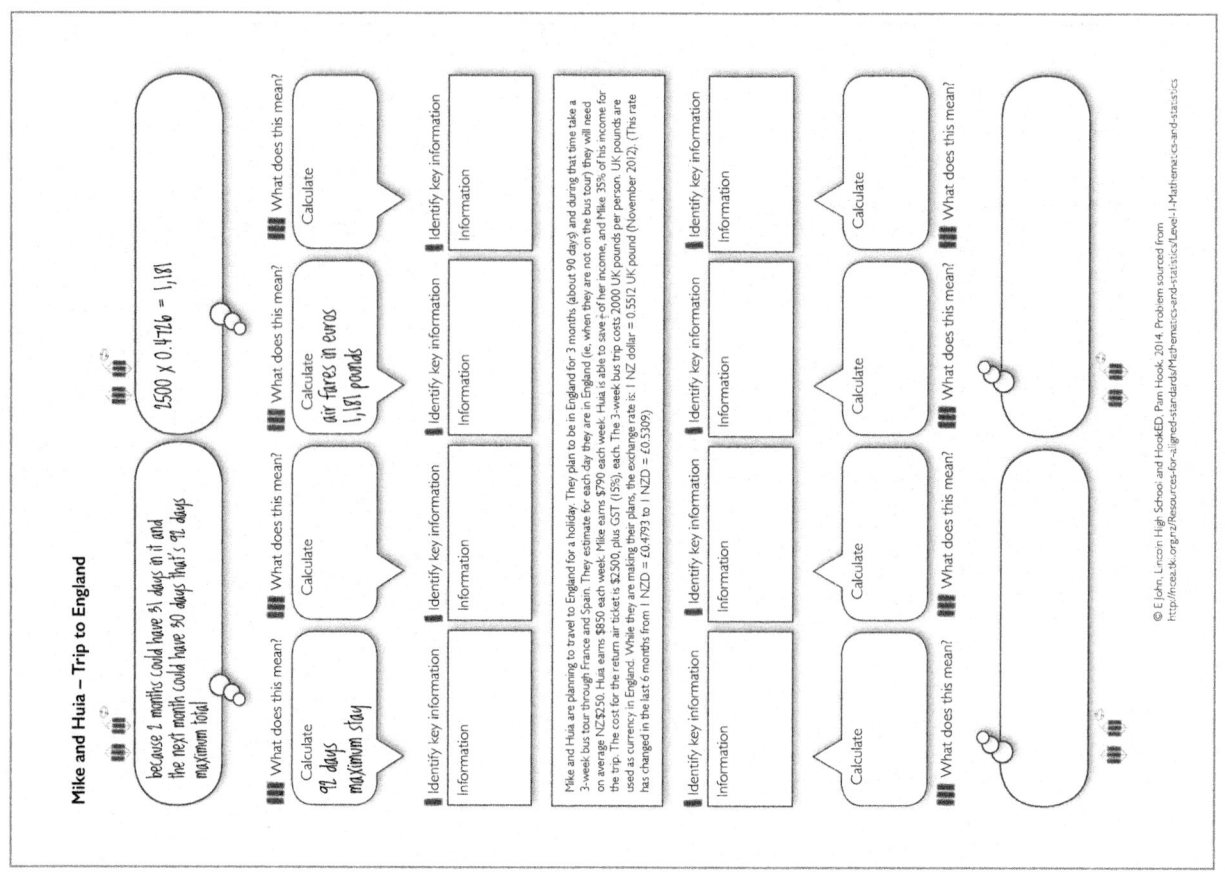

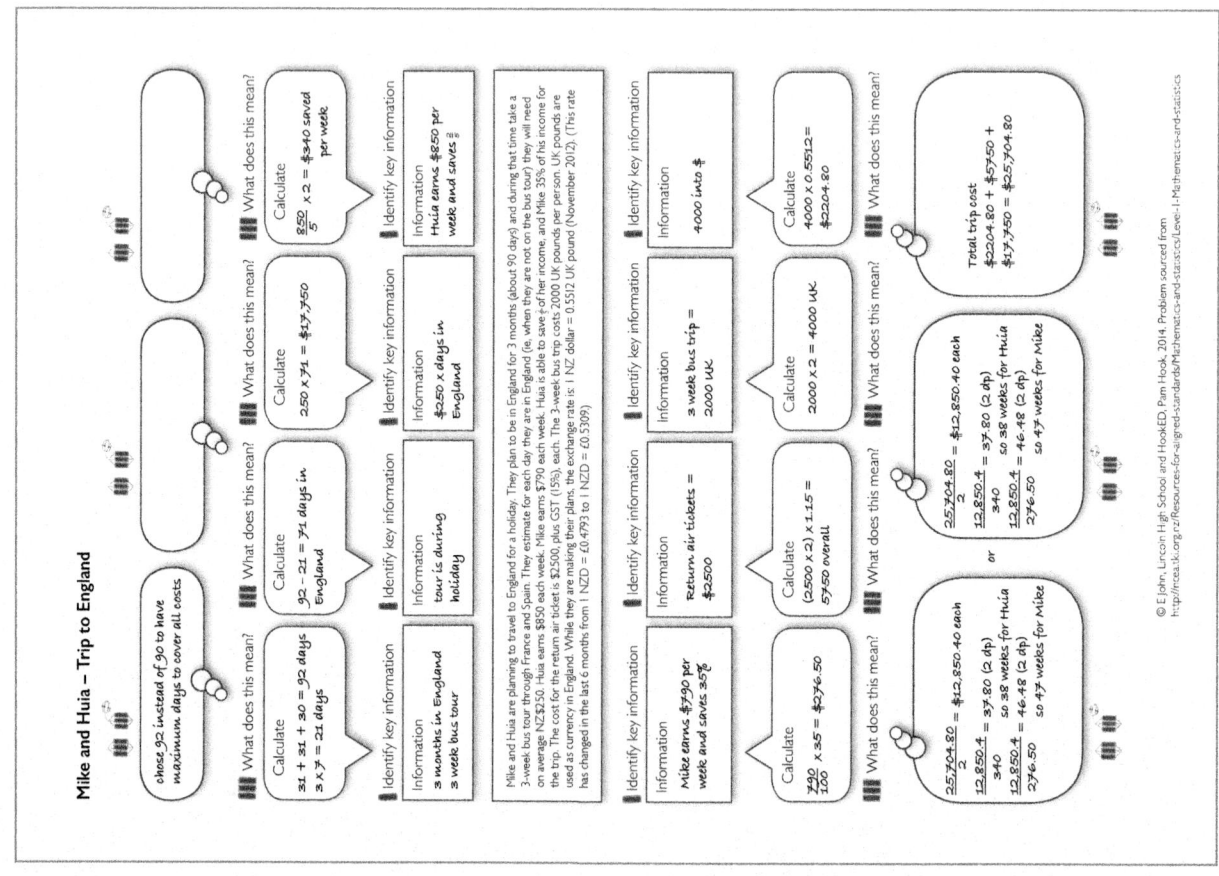

Figure 4.5: Student response to exam question

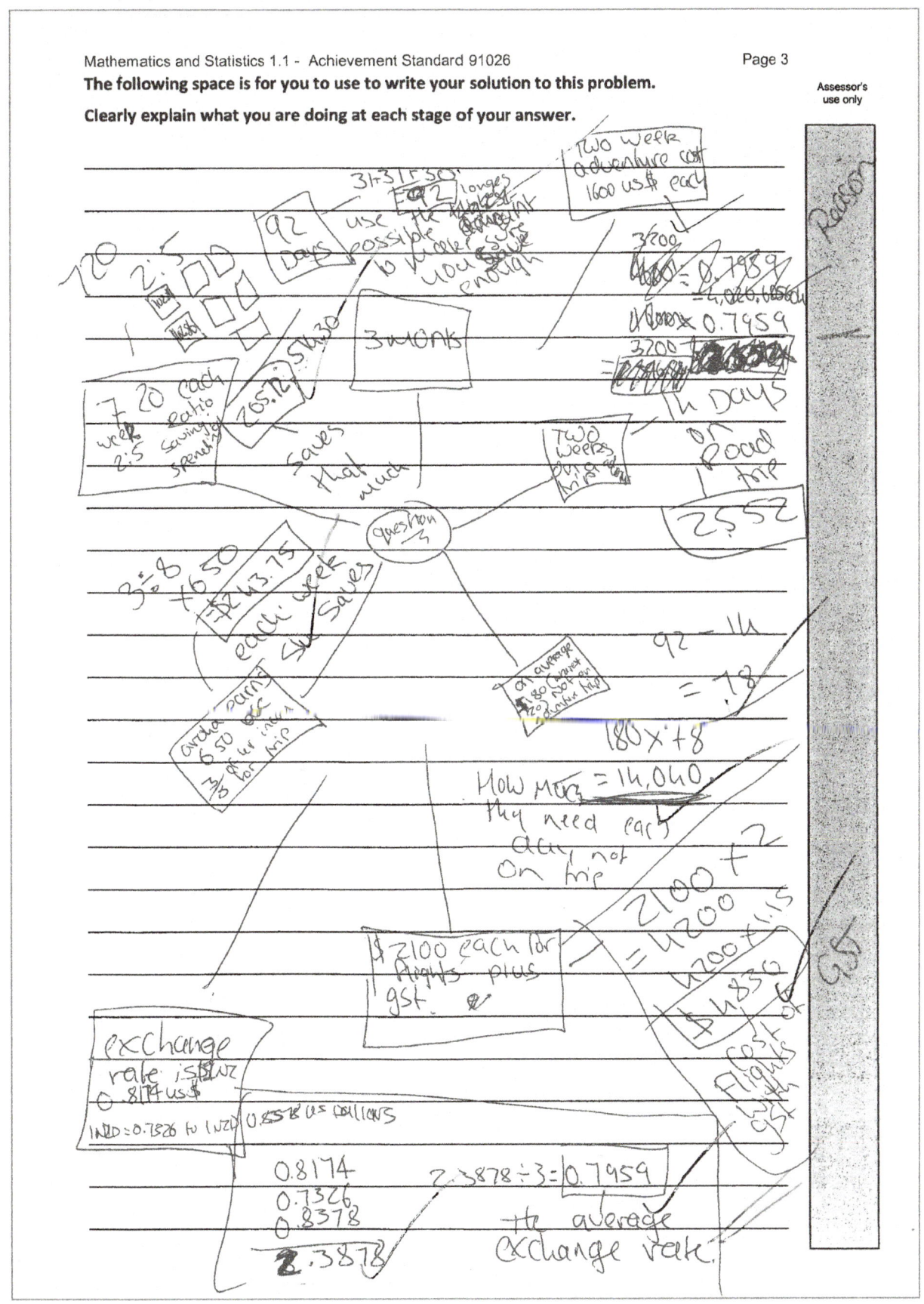

Self assessment rubric

Template 4.1: Self assessment rubric for numerical reasoning

SOLO level	SOLO explanation	Assessment		
		Student	Peer	Teacher
Prestructural	I need help to identify the key information in a complex maths problem.			
Unistructural	I can identify the key information in a maths problem.			
Multistructural	I can identify the key information in a maths problem and work out (calculate) what the information means.			
Relational	I can combine the information in a logical sequence to solve the maths problem.			
Extended abstract	I can extend my understanding of the problem by identifying the variables in the key information and/or using the logical process to deduce a proof or generalised rule.			

Key benefits

The following are some of the key benefits of using the Describe ++ map (along with the Describe + map if needed for scaffolding) in mathematics teaching:

- Students are prepared to try increasingly more complex questions once they can see how to use the structure of the Describe ++ map to break down their thinking.
- The structure of the Describe + and Describe ++ maps encourages students to show their working.
- By starting to unpack a problem using the Describe + map, students can demonstrate multistructural (NCEA Achieved) skills and relational (NCEA Merit) skills.
- The Describe ++ map helps develop student thinking about the extended abstract (Excellence) requirements of complex questions. For example, the "What if?" thought bubbles prompt students to consider variations within the question (eg, the exchange rate) and discuss what effect these variations might have on the final answer.

5. SOLO Hexagons

SOLO Hexagons offer a strategy for generating and connecting ideas. Working individually, in pairs or in collaborative groups, students may do any of the following:
- brainstorm everything they know about a given topic (presented as a focus question)
- record each idea or thought on a separate blank hexagon
- arrange their ideas by tessellating the hexagons.

Alternatively the teacher or other students may supply the content ideas on the hexagons.

The outcome differs according to the SOLO level:

 In a **multistructural** outcome, students can justify (talk about or annotate) the individual hexagons.

 In a **relational** outcome, students can make straight-edge connections between simple hexagon sequences, tessellate the hexagons (making connections) and explain why they have linked the ideas in this way.

 In an **extended abstract** outcome, students can explore the node where three hexagons share a corner and make a generalisation about the nature of the relationship between the ideas.

HookED SOLO Hexagon Generator

You can create your own topic SOLO Hexagons in this way:

1. Go to www.pamhook.com, click on *SOLO apps* and find the SOLO Hexagon Generator.
2. Enter the terms you want to display on the hexagons.
3. Click on Generate Document.

Your hexagons are then presented in a Word document, where you can input any equations and symbols you would like to add and change the size of the font.

When designing learning activities using the HookED SOLO Hexagon Generator, bear in mind that it takes time to cut out each hexagon, unless you have already prepared cut-out hexagons.

How are SOLO Hexagons used?

SOLO Hexagons are a versatile tool for the mathematics classroom, allowing teachers to clearly identify students' prior knowledge, misconceptions and creative approaches. This section shows how you can use them as a diagnostic tool in a pre-test activity and/or for formative and summative assessment.

Pre-test activity: Fractions

This first example of a pre-test activity describes a structured approach to using SOLO Hexagons; the next example (focused on measurement) is more open ended.

In this example, we gave students three sets of hexagons, covering fractions; improper fractions; and mixed fractions and fraction pictures (Figures 5.1–5.3). You could give more able students the algebraic fraction set as well (Figure 5.4).

Step 1: The first task was for students to sort the hexagons into groups and explain their decisions, supported by the SOLO Describe map (Figure 5.5). Students can complete these activities individually or in small groups (see Figure 5.13 in the student examples section) or – something we found worked well – they can start the activities individually and then complete them as a group.

© Essential Resources Educational Publishers Ltd

Figure 5.1: SOLO Hexagons for proper fractions

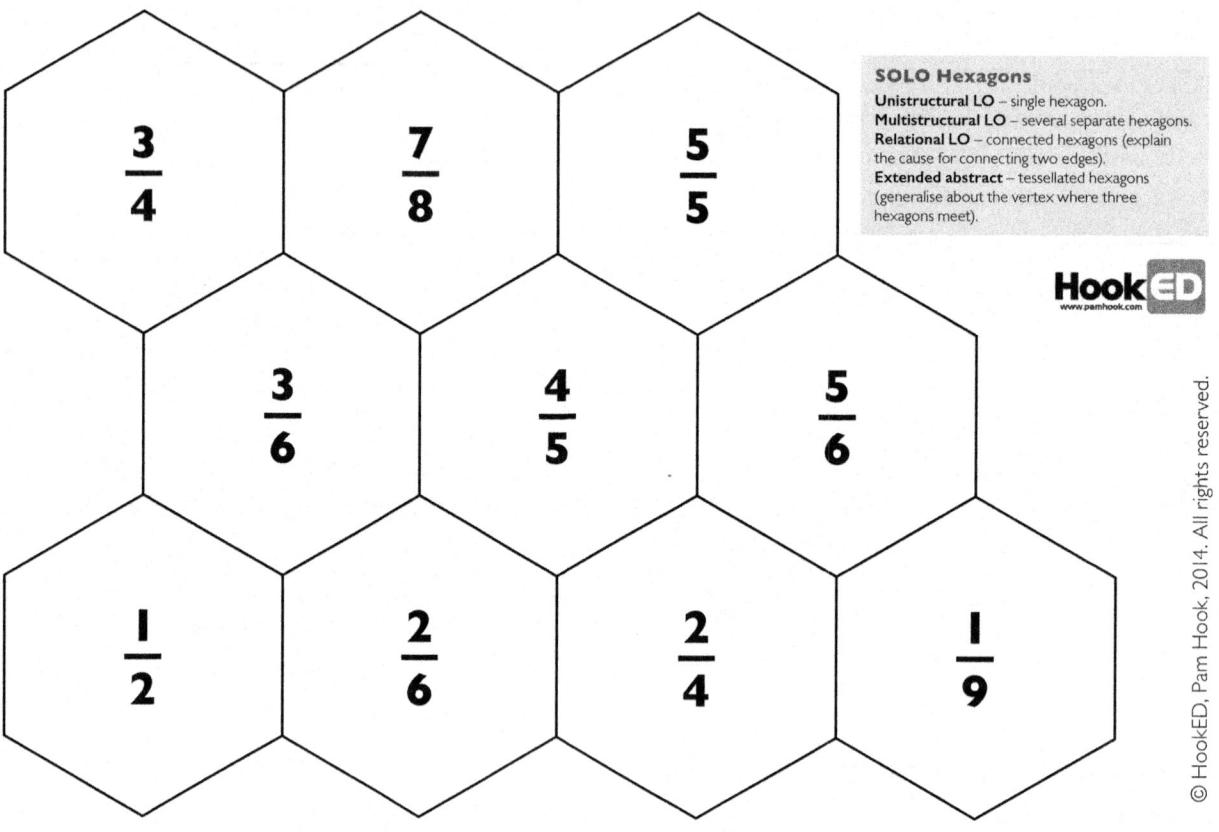

Figure 5.2: SOLO Hexagons for improper fractions

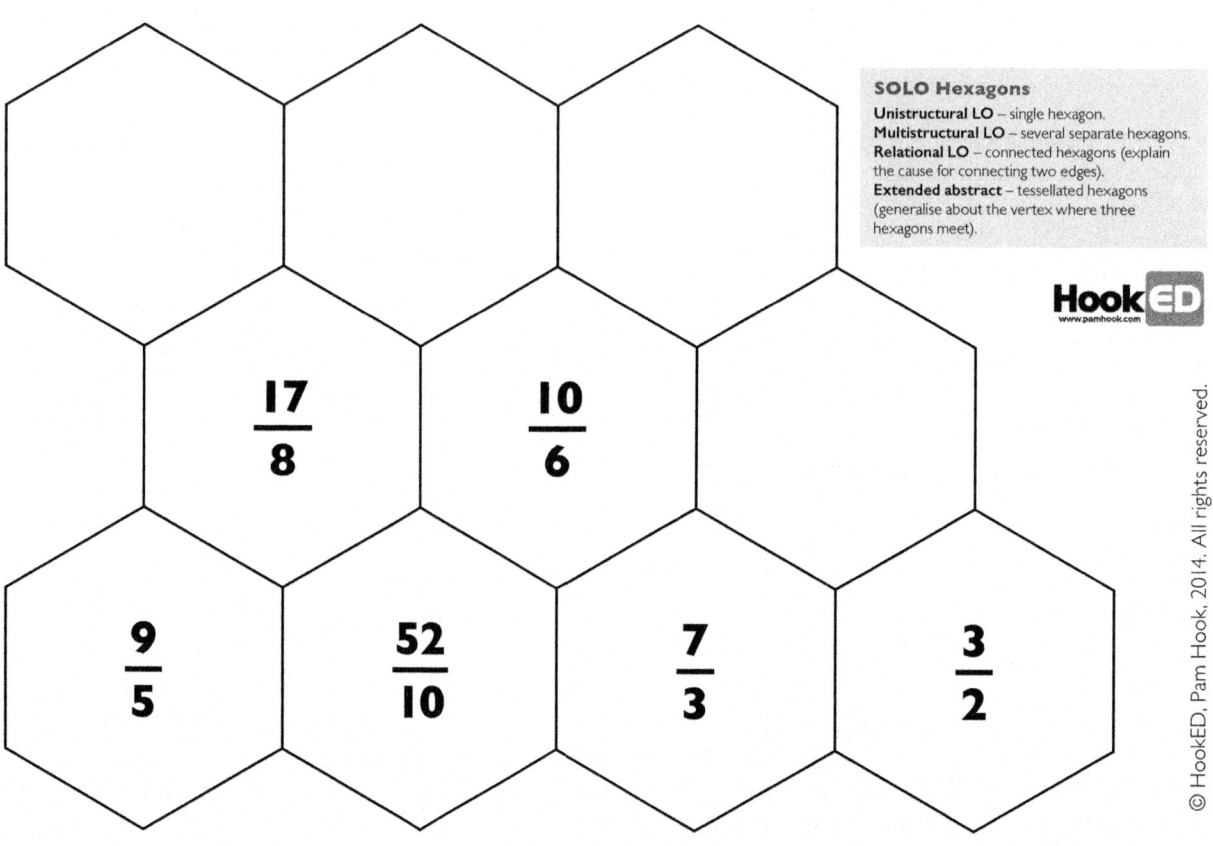

Figure 5.3: SOLO Hexagons for mixed fractions and picture fractions

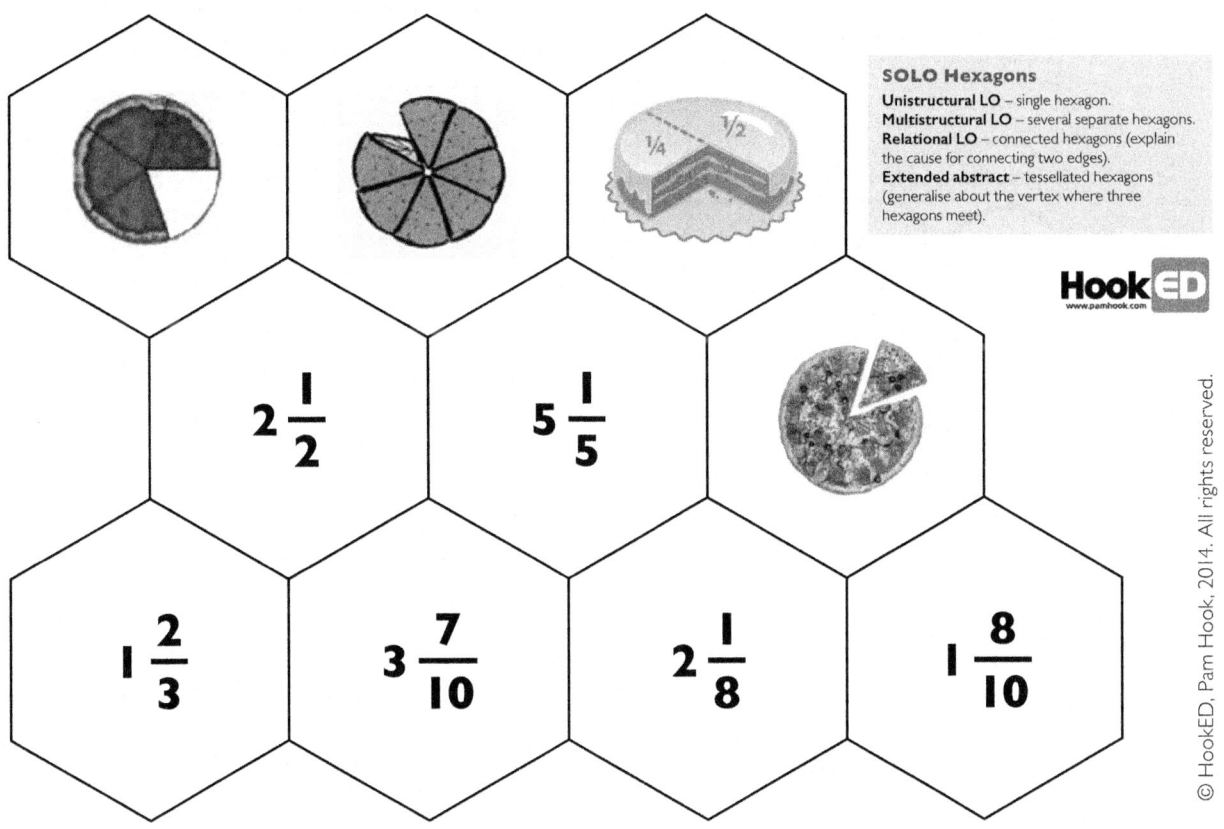

Figure 5.4: SOLO Hexagons for algebraic fractions

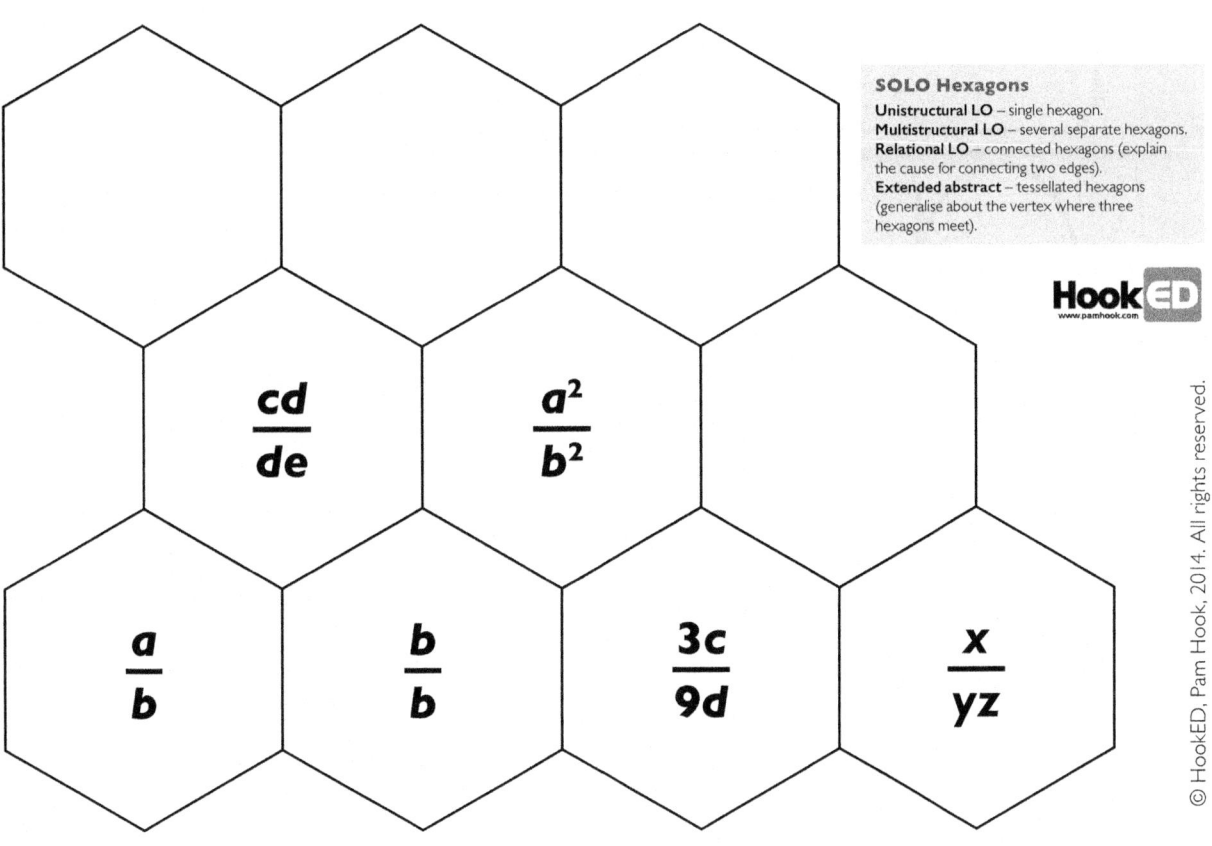

Figure 5.5: SOLO Describe map for fraction groups

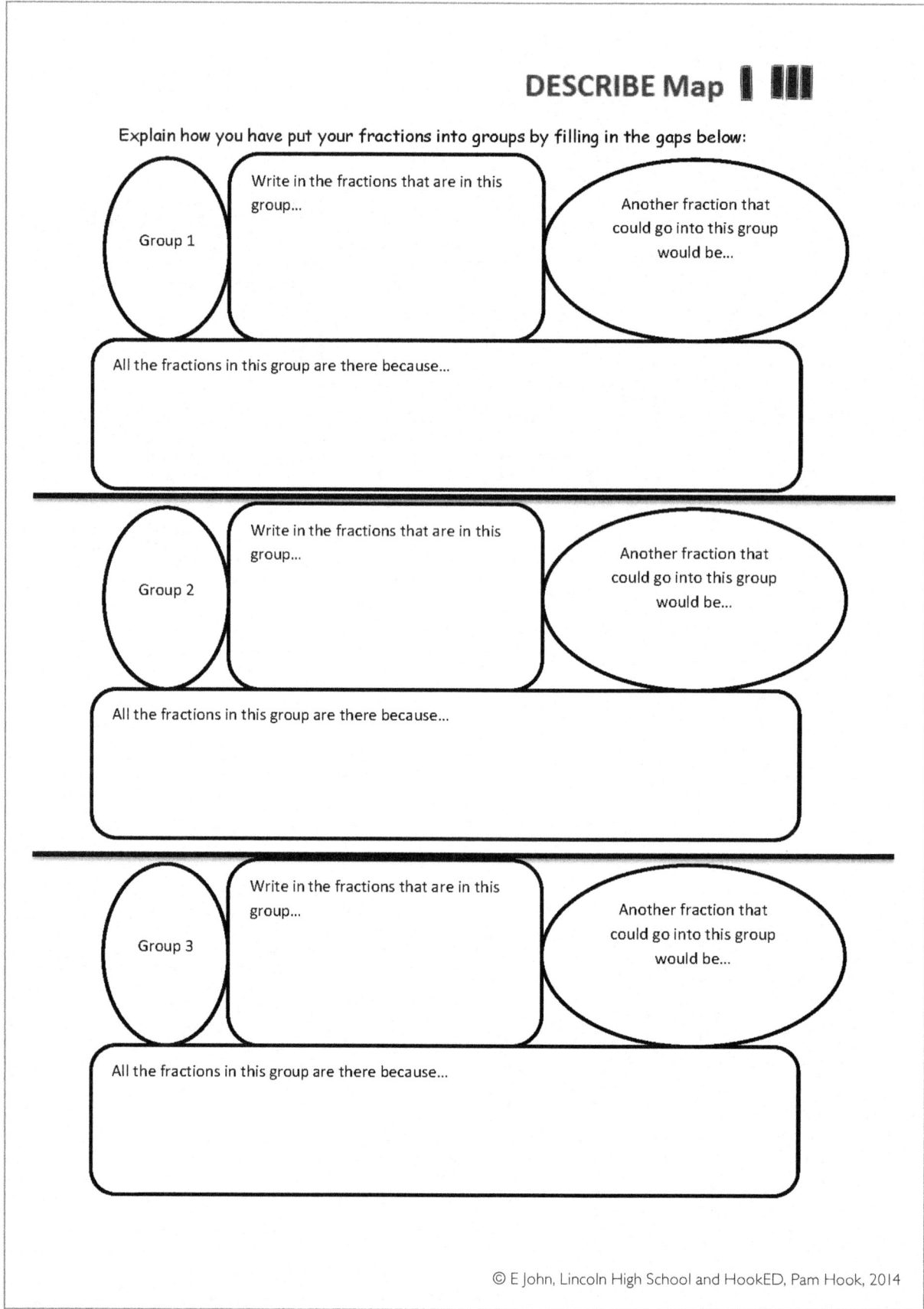

Step 2: We asked the students to write any questions they now had about fractions. These questions were full of good information and helped inform our teaching for our fractions topic. Here are some examples:

> I wonder what $\frac{8}{8}$ looks like.
>
> I wonder what's the point of fractions with both numbers the same – writing a whole would be easier.
>
> I wonder what the best way to say fractions like $\frac{52}{10}$ is.
>
> I wonder why there is an extra number beside the fraction.

Starting off with this activity, rather than starting with a pre-test that has to be marked quickly or just jumping straight into the topic, made it easier for us identify students' misconceptions, what they were comfortable with, their prior knowledge and what they understood thoroughly enough to explain.

Follow-up (extension): Figure 5.6 presents a SOLO Compare and Contrast map as a useful follow-up, where students look across the different sets of fractions to identify their similarities and differences.

Figure 5.6: SOLO Compare and Contrast map for fraction groups

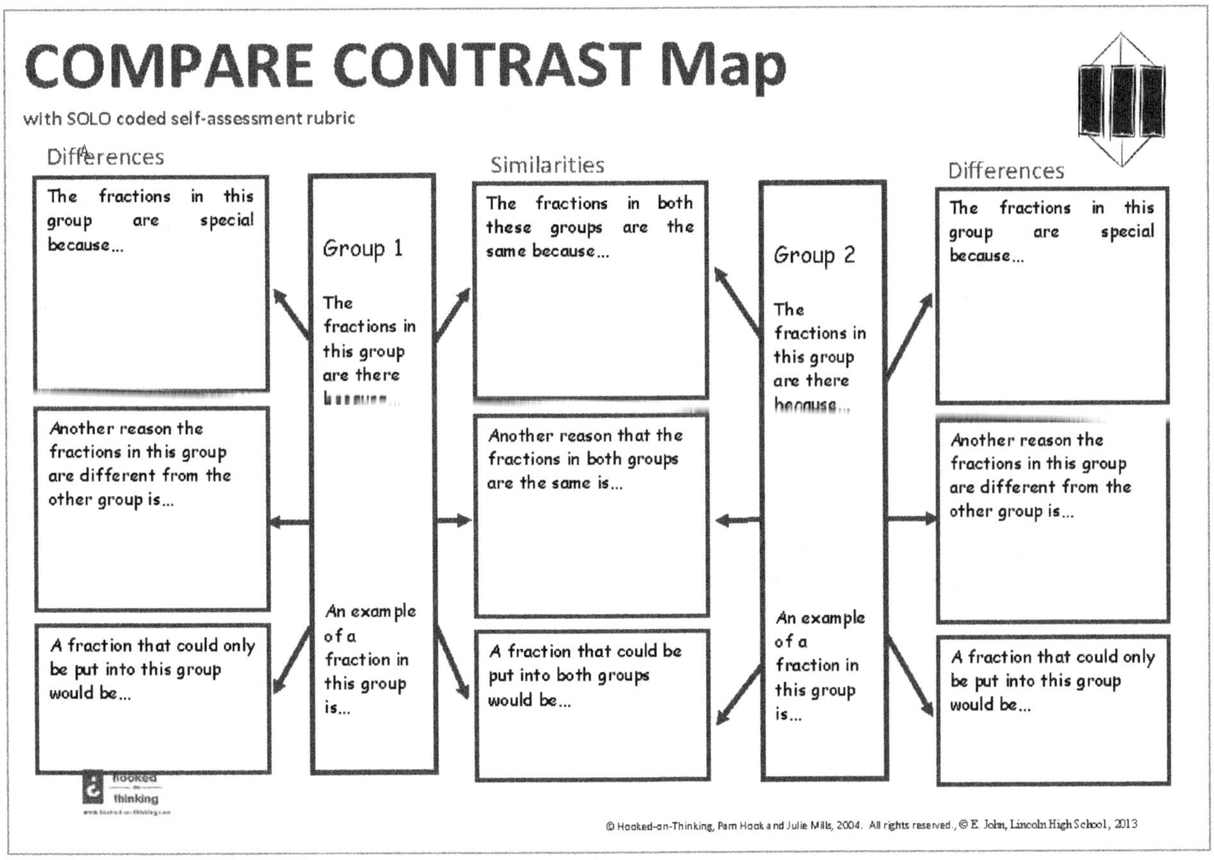

COMPARE CONTRAST Map
with SOLO coded self-assessment rubric

Differences		Similarities		Differences
The fractions in this group are special because…	Group 1 — The fractions in this group are there because…	The fractions in both these groups are the same because…	Group 2 — The fractions in this group are there because…	The fractions in this group are special because…
Another reason the fractions in this group are different from the other group is…		Another reason that the fractions in both groups are the same is…		Another reason the fractions in this group are different from the other group is…
A fraction that could only be put into this group would be…	An example of a fraction in this group is…	A fraction that could be put into both groups would be…	An example of a fraction in this group is…	A fraction that could only be put into this group would be…

© Hooked-on-Thinking, Pam Hook and Julie Mills, 2004. All rights reserved., © E. John, Lincoln High School, 2013

Pre-test activity: Measurement

This example demonstrates a more open-ended approach to using SOLO Hexagons.

Step 1: We gave students blank hexagons and asked them to write any units they knew on the hexagons.

Step 2: Students again sorted the hexagons into groups and explained their sorting using a Describe map similar to the one used in the fraction activity (Figure 5.7; see also Figures 5.14 and 5.15 in the student examples section).

Step 3: We asked students to add the following units to their arrangement: litre, millilitre, hectare, tonne, ton, cm^2, mm^3. This again opened up informative conversations among the students and between the students and the teacher. Students often sorted units by linking them to how they were used in everyday life – for example, in the context of cooking, distances or time. Allowing the students to link to contexts they were familiar with at the beginning of the topic made it easy to engage students and gave them ownership of their learning.

Figure 5.7: SOLO Describe map for measurement

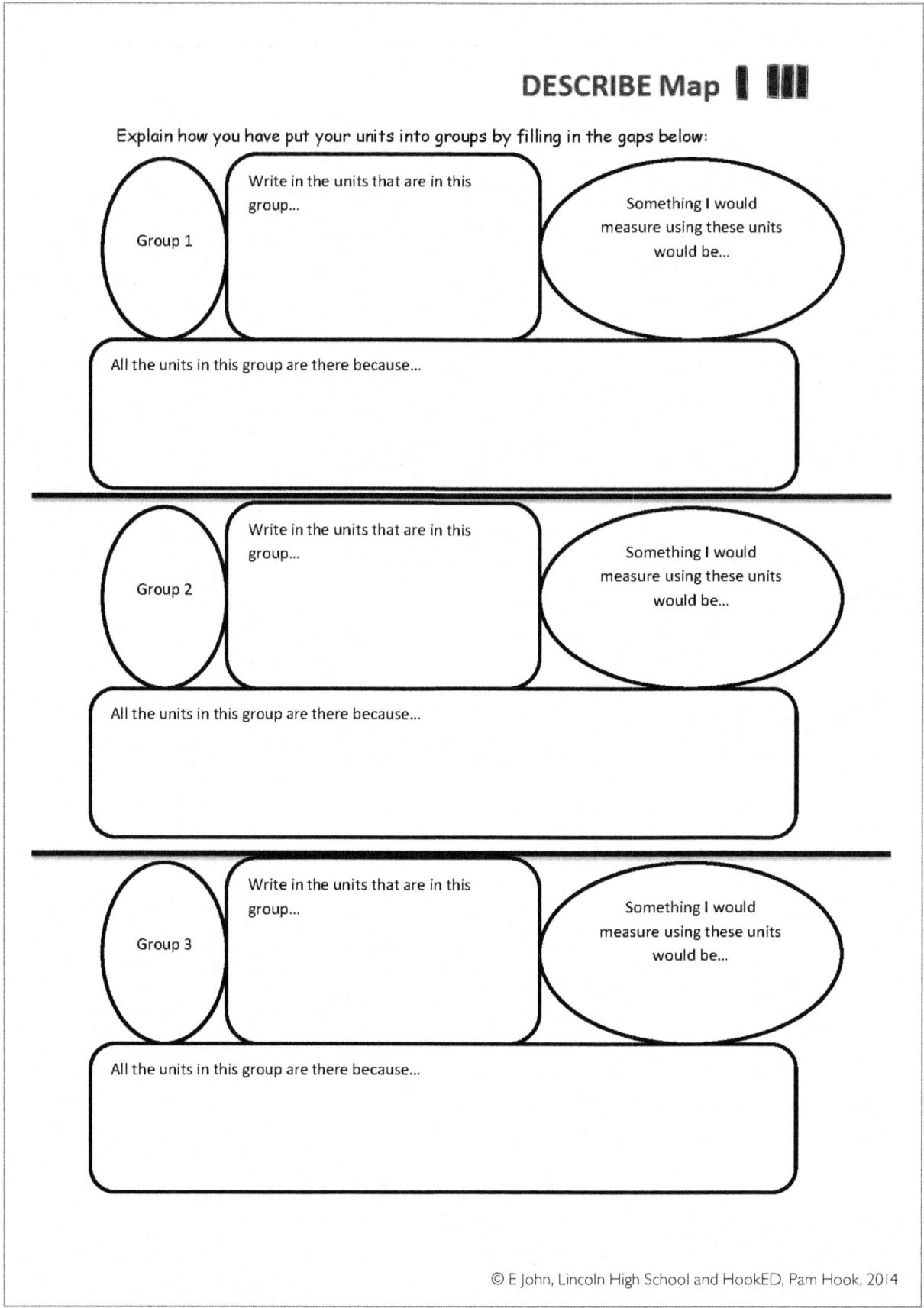

Collaborative activity for formative assessment: Fractions, decimals, percentages

For our topic on converting between fractions, decimals and percentages, we started with a sorting activity similar to the fraction pre-test activity (see above). Figure 5.8 shows the content of this activity.

This initial sorting made it easier to put students into home groups and expert groups that had a good range of abilities. In their expert groups students were expected to explain two different ways to complete their particular conversion (eg, converting fractions to decimals). They were also given three to four different numbers to convert into the other form to check their understanding (Figure 5.9).

Figure 5.8: Content for SOLO Hexagons activity on fractions, decimals and percentages

50%	0.5	$\frac{1}{2}$	$\frac{30}{60}$	
33.$\dot{3}$%	0.$\dot{3}$	$\frac{1}{3}$	$\frac{7}{21}$	
25%	0.25	$\frac{1}{4}$	$\frac{5}{20}$	
30%	0.3	$\frac{3}{10}$	$\frac{90}{300}$	
250%	2.5	$\frac{5}{2}$	$\frac{30}{12}$	
72%	0.72	$\frac{72}{100}$	$\frac{18}{25}$	
720%	7.2	$7\frac{1}{5}$	$\frac{36}{5}$	
0.3%	0.003	$\frac{3}{1\,000}$	$\frac{600}{200\,000}$	

$\frac{600}{200\,000}$	2.5	50%	$\frac{5}{20}$	
0.$\dot{3}$	$\frac{18}{25}$		$\frac{3}{10}$	720%
	25%	$\frac{30}{12}$	0.5	$\frac{1}{3}$
30%	$\frac{3}{1\,000}$	0.72		$7\frac{1}{5}$
$\frac{72}{100}$		$\frac{7}{21}$	0.3%	0.25
	33.$\dot{3}$%	$\frac{1}{4}$	0.$\dot{3}$	$\frac{5}{2}$
$\frac{30}{60}$	72%		$\frac{36}{5}$	0.003
250%	$\frac{90}{300}$	$\frac{1}{2}$	7.2	

© Essential Resources Educational Publishers Ltd

Figure 5.9: Sample method sheets for converting between fractions, decimals and percentages

---

Fractions → Decimals

Method 1:
Get an equivalent fraction with 100 as the denominator

$\frac{1}{4} = \frac{25}{100} = 0.25$ or $\frac{7}{50} = \frac{14}{100} = 0.14$

Method 2:
Calculator method

$\frac{7}{21} = 7 \div 21 = 0.\dot{3}$

Method 3:

Practice Examples – can you do these?
1. $\frac{1}{10} =$
2. $\frac{3}{10} =$
3. $\frac{5}{2} =$

Percentage → Decimals

Method 1:
Take the percentage and divide it by 100

30% = 30 ÷ 100 = 0.3

Method 2:
Move the numbers around the decimal point 2 times.

65% = 65. = 0.65

Method 3:

Practice Examples
1. 22% =
2. 74.3% =
3. 162% =
4. 0.12% =

Decimals → Fractions

Method 1:
Put the same number of zeroes in the denominator as there are decimal places

$0.72 = \frac{72}{100}$ $1.392 = \frac{1392}{1000}$ or $1\frac{392}{1000}$

Then you can simplify if possible

Method 2:
Calculator Method
Enter the decimal into your calculator and push equals. Then push your fraction key (a b/c)

$0.72 = \frac{18}{25}$ if will simplify the fraction

Method 3:

Practice Examples
1. 0.85 =
2. 0.19 =
3. 2.43 =
4. 0.003 =

Decimals → Percentage

Method 1:
Multiply the decimal by 100

0.82 × 100 = 82%

Method 2:
Move the numbers around the decimal point 2 times.

0.65 = 0.65 = 65%

Method 3:

Practice Examples
1. 0.44 =
2. 0.389 =
3. 4.17 =
4. 0.003 =

Figure 5.9: Sample method sheets for converting between fractions, decimals and percentages (continued)

Percentage → Fractions

Method 1:
Put the percentage over 100.

$79\% = \frac{79}{100}$

Method 2:
Change to a decimal and then convert to a fraction.

$20\% = 0.2 = \frac{2}{10}$

Method 3:

Practice Examples
1. 56% =

2. 81.5% =

3. 199% =

4. 0.12% =

If students were not sure how to do their particular conversion, we gave them one or two methods to master. Once the expert groups were confident with making their given conversion, group members returned to their home groups where they had to teach their conversion to the others.

With this activity, we found that students in their expert groups asked questions they wouldn't have asked otherwise, as they had to be the expert and wanted to make sure they were passing on correct information. In addition, this collaborative activity allowed for all students to contribute, whatever their level of ability in this topic. If you have access to mini whiteboards, they are a useful tool for students to share their knowledge in the home groups.

Summative assessment: Fraction sum-up activity

SOLO Hexagons can be adapted to explore students' understanding at the end of a topic, as in this example of an end-of-unit activity.

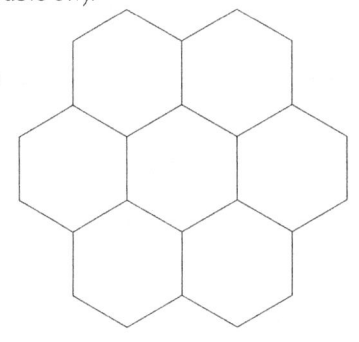

We gave students the fraction sum-up activity sheet (Figure 5.10) and asked them to:
- choose six fractions from a list of 10 (Figure 5.11)
- write each chosen fraction on one of the hexagons on the adapted hexagon activity sheet
- follow the prompts to complete the operations noted on the activity sheet and show all working
- use extra sheets if you need more room to complete the centre hexagon
- check your outcomes against the SOLO self assessment question prompts (Table 5.1).

The speech bubble prompts in the activity sheet emphasise showing working. In the past, we have had issues with students resisting showing their working when doing calculations, but with this activity resistance was not an issue.

Figure 5.10: End-of-unit fraction sum-up activity sheet

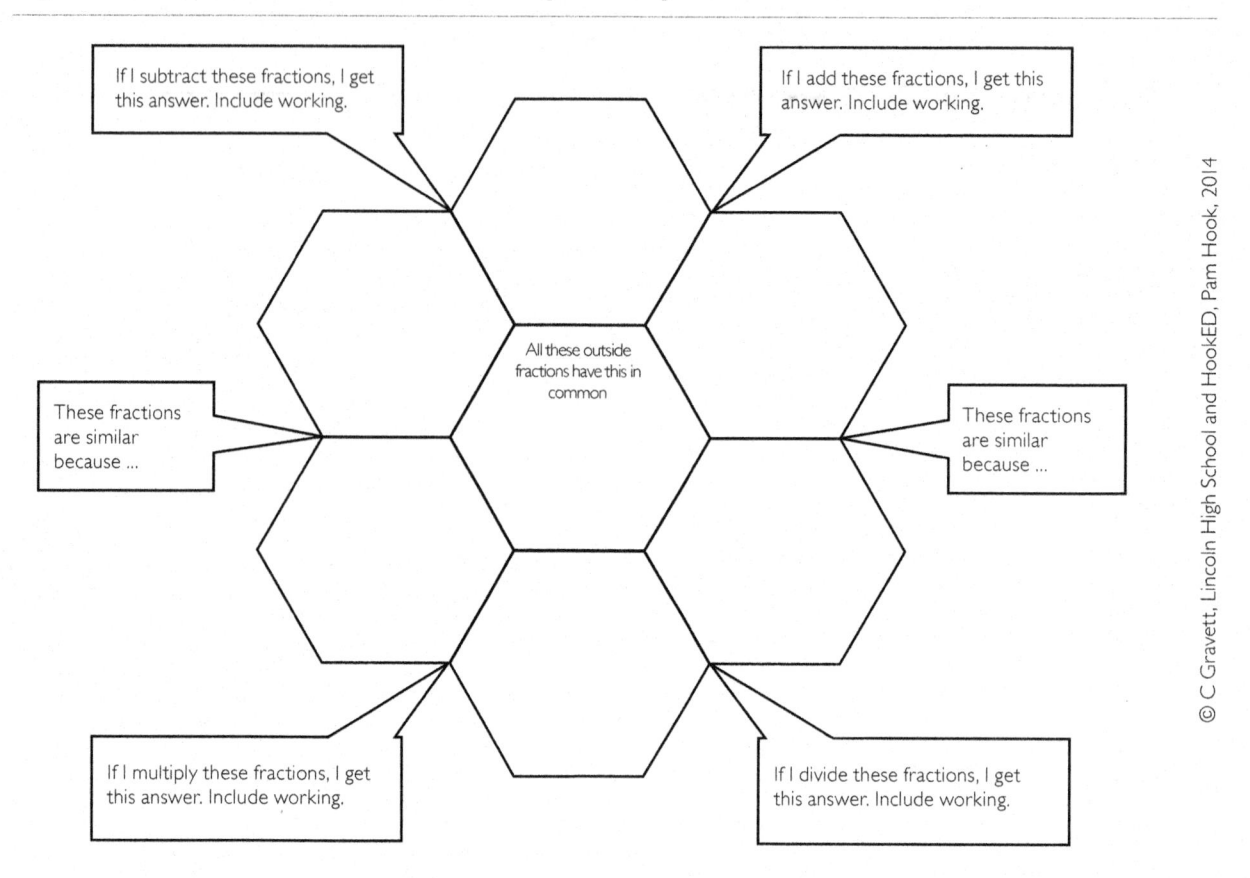

If I subtract these fractions, I get this answer. Include working.

If I add these fractions, I get this answer. Include working.

All these outside fractions have this in common

These fractions are similar because ...

These fractions are similar because ...

If I multiply these fractions, I get this answer. Include working.

If I divide these fractions, I get this answer. Include working.

Figure 5.11: List of fractions for fraction sum-up activity

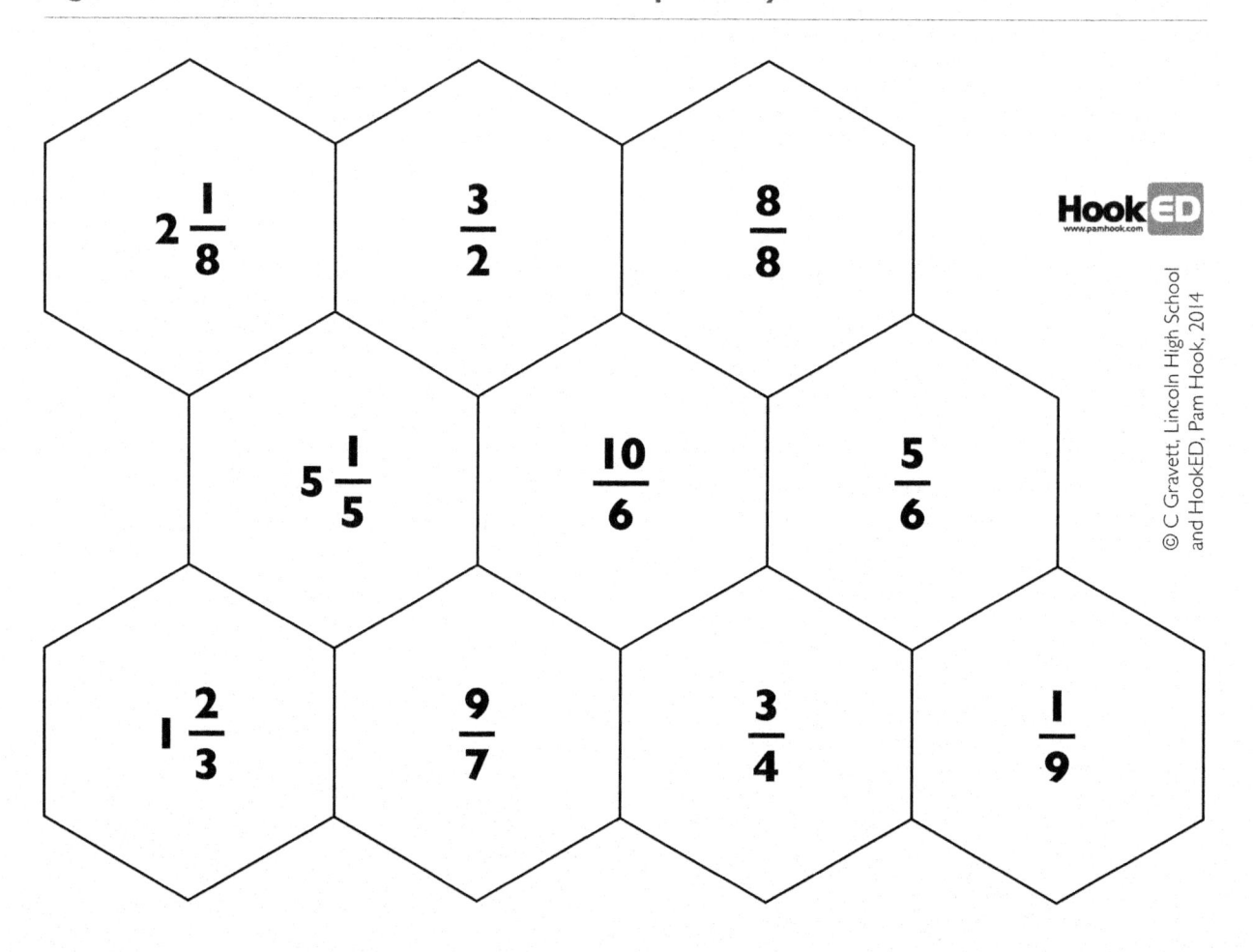

$2\frac{1}{8}$

$\frac{3}{2}$

$\frac{8}{8}$

$5\frac{1}{5}$

$\frac{10}{6}$

$\frac{5}{6}$

$1\frac{2}{3}$

$\frac{9}{7}$

$\frac{3}{4}$

$\frac{1}{9}$

40 © Essential Resources Educational Publishers Ltd

Table 5.1: Fractions question prompt rubric

Question prompt	SOLO level
Can I complete one of the operations with working?	Unistructural
Can I complete any of the operations with working? Can I find connections between any of the fractions besides fraction types?	Multistructural
Can I find connections between any of the fractions that require further calculations?	Relational
Can I find a connection with all the fractions? Does this connection require further investigation than what I have already completed? Have I clearly described this connection?	Extended abstract

At the end of the activity, students had an opportunity to reach the extended abstract level by trying to link all six of their fractions together in some way. Students may need more space than the small hexagon in the middle to complete this task.

The benefits of doing a summative assessment in this format are that:
- it is fairly quick to mark
- it is easy to identify areas students need to work on.

We would recommend doing some activities to familiarise students with this format before using it in a test. An effective way to prepare is to do starters with fractions in a triangle formation and a specified action on each side and then prompt students for a connection between all three (Figure 5.12).

Figure 5.12: Assessment preparation diagram

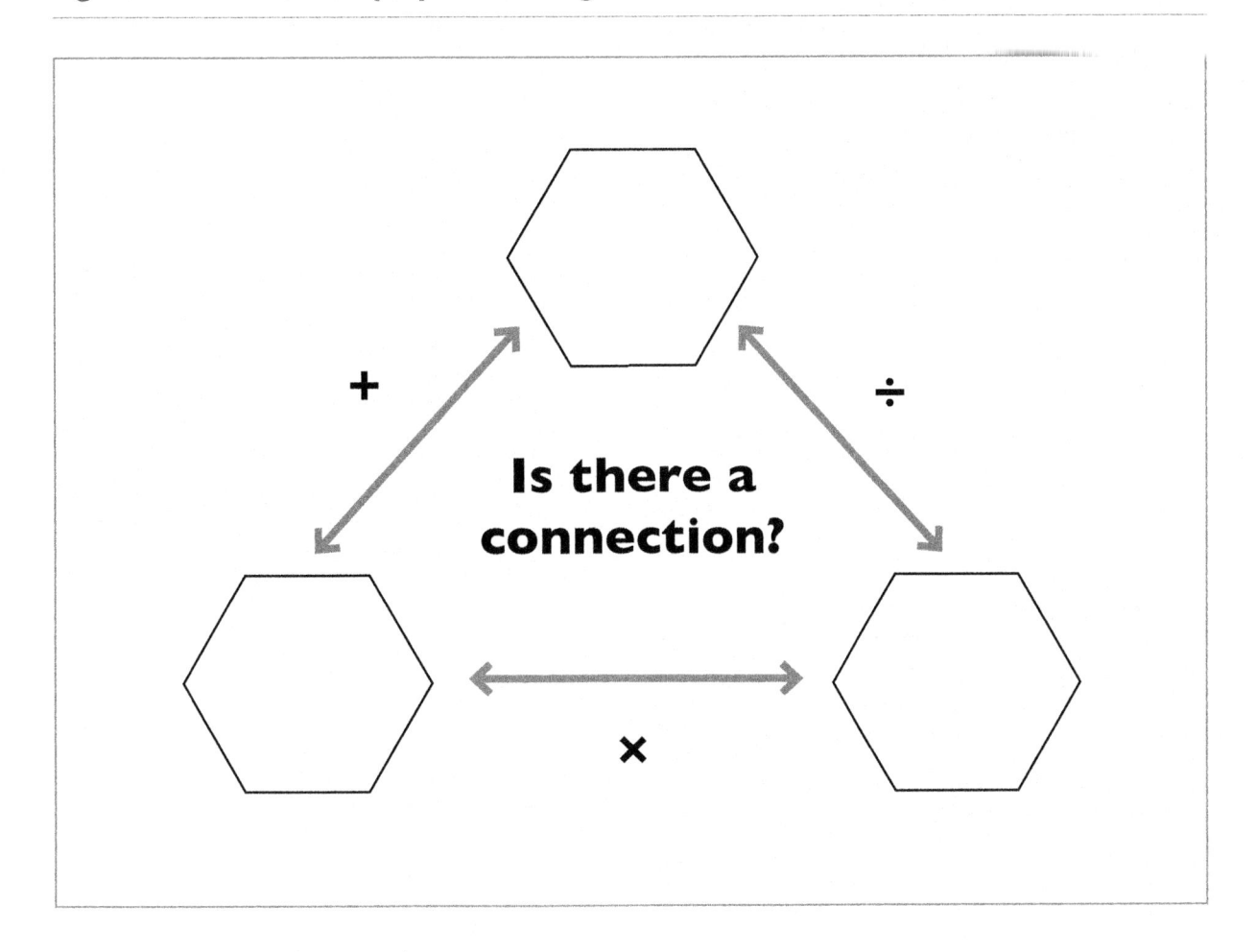

Student examples

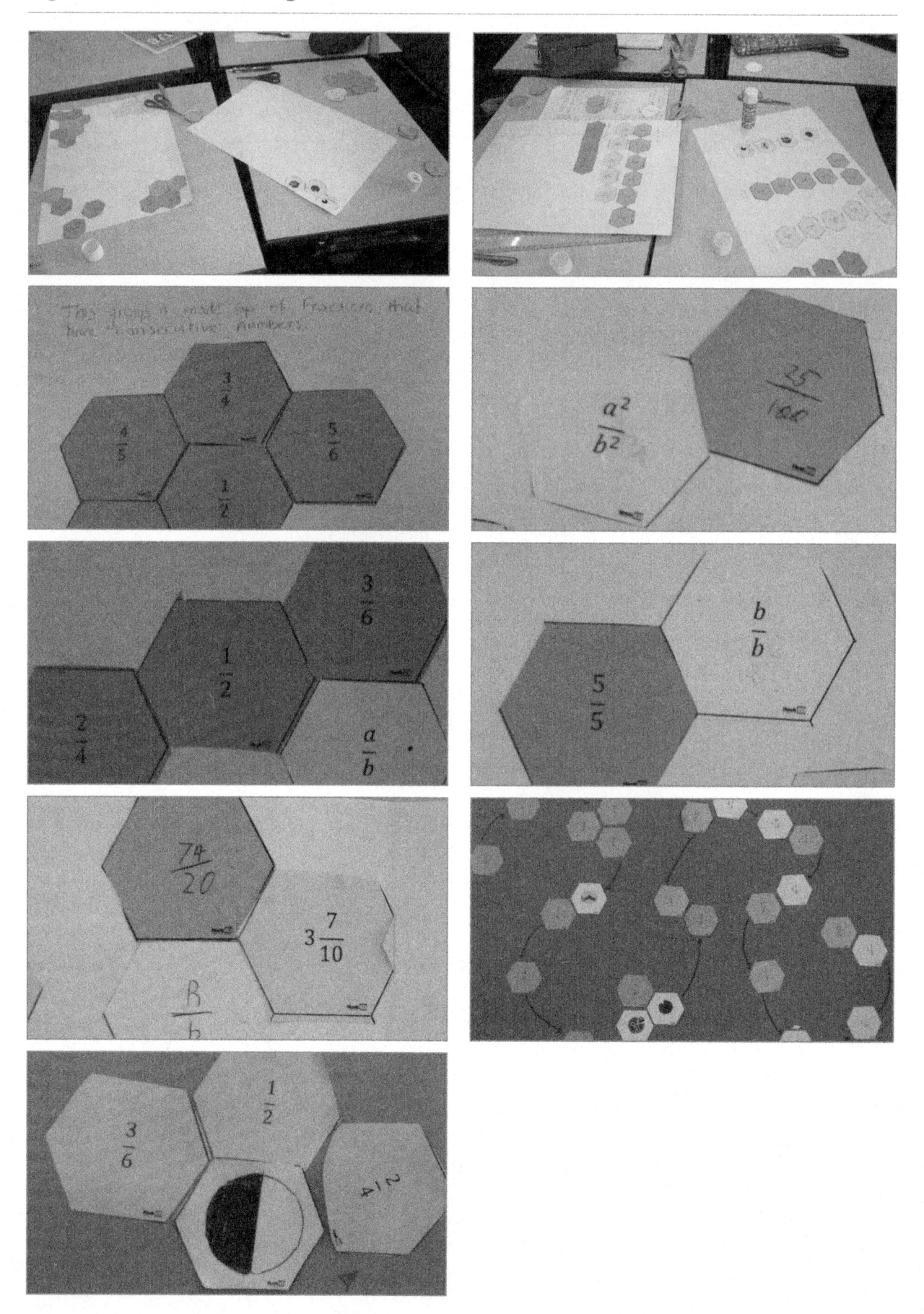

Figure 5.13: Prior knowledge of fractions

Figure 5.14: Prior knowledge of measurement

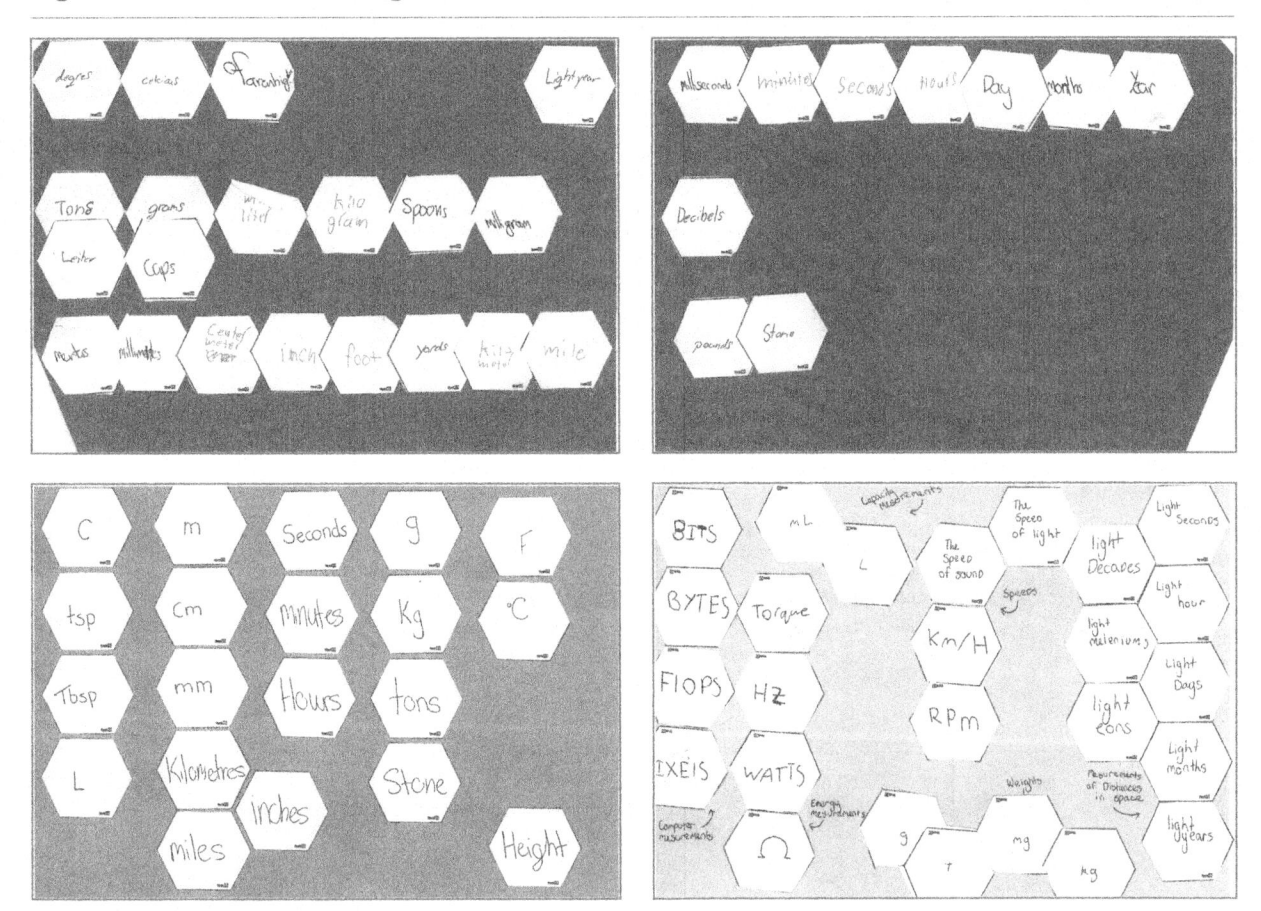

Figure 5.15: Student response to SOLO Describe map for measurement

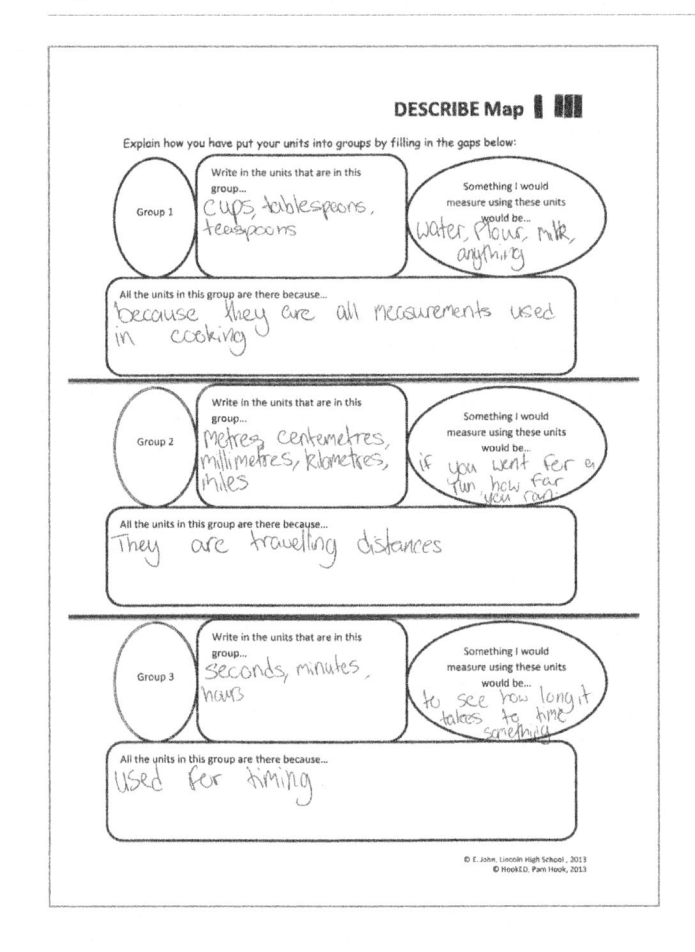

43

Self assessment rubric

Template 5.1: Self assessment rubric for linking mathematical ideas

SOLO level	SOLO explanation	Assessment		
		Student	Peer	Teacher
Prestructural	I struggle to identify mathematical ideas on the SOLO Hexagons.			
Unistructural	I can identify a relevant mathematical idea on a SOLO Hexagon.			
Multistructural	I can identify several relevant mathematical ideas on the SOLO Hexagons.			
Relational	I can make links between mathematical ideas on different SOLO Hexagons and explain (give reasons for/ show working to justify) these links …			
Extended abstract	… and I can make a generalisation about the nature of the mathematical relationships and/or wonder about their variability.			

Key benefits

The following are some of the key benefits of using SOLO Hexagons in mathematics teaching:
- They enhance versatile thinking across a wide range of mathematical content areas and contexts (not just the topics discussed in this book).
- Students can engage their mathematical reasoning using their prior knowledge.
- The learning design of SOLO Hexagons sets up activities with multiple entry points, so your students will not be left saying "I can't start".
- SOLO Hexagons allow students to explore connections and ideas their teacher may not have foreseen.
- Once students have used SOLO Hexagons in the classroom, they can use them as an additional study tool for their own revision.

Conclusion

The SOLO Taxonomy levels and the SOLO strategies and approaches described in this book have been effective in enhancing student outcomes in mathematics classrooms. The SOLO functioning and declarative knowledge rubrics, SOLO Hexagons, the HookED SOLO Describe ++ map and the problem solving strategies can be (and are being) used to make learning outcomes visible in number and algebra, geometry and measurement and in statistical investigations, probability and statistical literacy. Having SOLO as a model of learning helps students make connections when thinking mathematically and provides objective criteria for self-assessing their learning outcomes. As the taxonomy is generic, these SOLO-based strategies can be applied comprehensively.

Additionally, when mathematics teachers adopt SOLO Taxonomy as a framework for designing and assessing learning activities (and the strategies used) in mathematics classrooms, we see a change in pedagogical approach. The conversation changes in the maths classroom. There is a greater emphasis on problem solving and pattern finding, and cognitive conflict aimed at challenging misconceptions and enhancing representations is introduced. Pedagogies of simple instrumental instruction correspondingly decline. It is our experience that these changes in pedagogical approach help students adopt a more flexible mental model about outcomes in maths, enhancing their ability to think more deeply about important mathematical constructs.

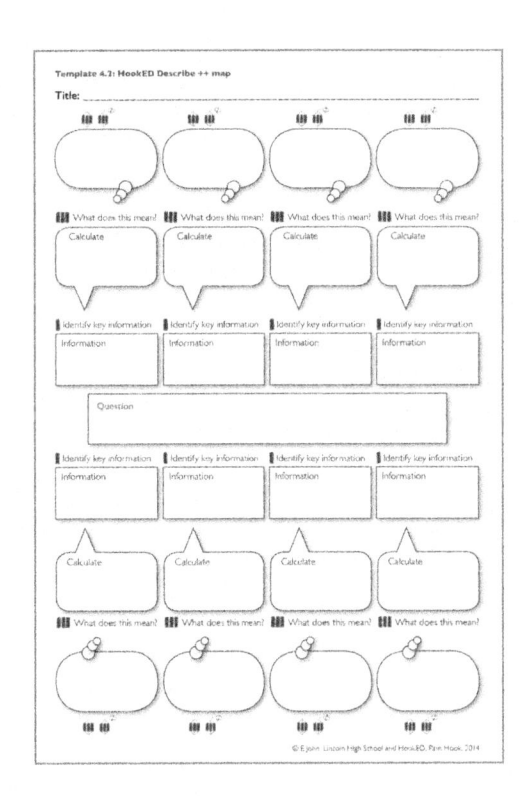

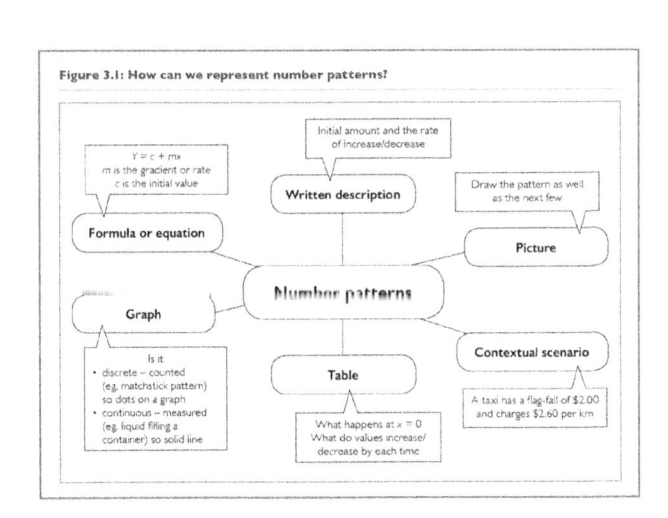

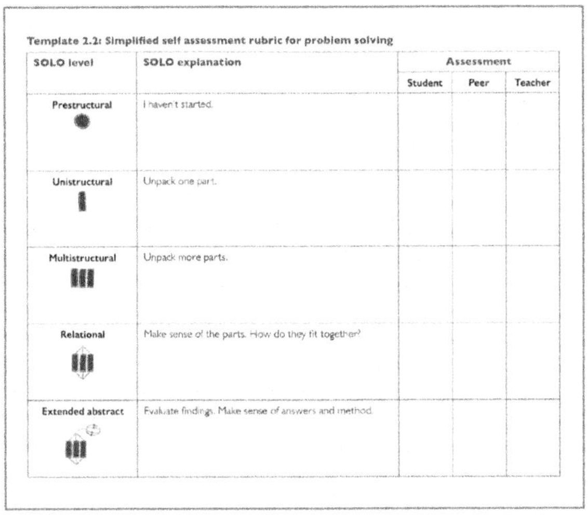

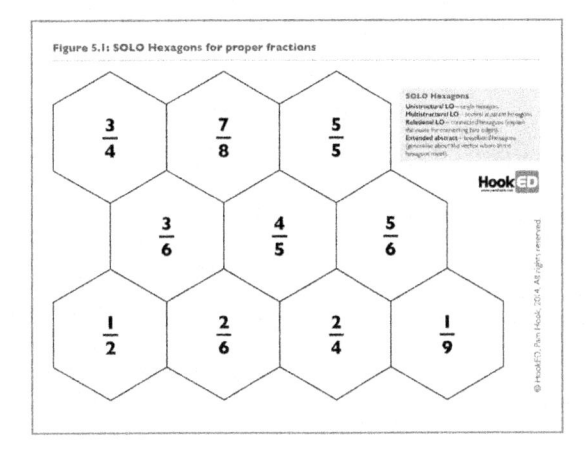

Further resources: A selection of SOLO self assessment rubrics

The following self assessment rubrics have been co-constructed for thinking in mathematical contexts. Specifically they cover a range of learning intentions (LIs) in the curriculum areas of:

- number and algebra
- geometry and measurement
- statistics.

SOLO rubrics in number and algebra

LI: Use appropriate methods/procedures to solve a problem

	Prestructural	Unistructural	Multistructural	Relational	Extended abstract
Use appropriate methods/ procedures	I need help to use appropriate methods. Example: Incorrect datum or process used	I can complete a single procedure if I am prompted or directed.	I can complete several procedures (similar and/or distinct) when attempting to solve a problem.	I can use these procedures in a logical sequence of steps to solve a problem. I can make connections between different methods/ procedures and the conceptual basis for the problem.	I can use these connections to devise a strategy to solve an unknown problem (one that lies outside of my previous experience).
Effective strategies [Insert strategies suggested by students and teachers]	Model. Show examples. Demonstrate. Give opportunity to practise. Reflect on outcomes. Use SOLO question prompts.	Give clear instructions. Prompt. Do situational teaching. Reflect on outcomes. Use SOLO question prompts.	Revisit, recap and remind. Reflect on outcomes. Use SOLO question prompts.	Give repeated opportunities to practise and reflect on outcomes. Use SOLO question prompts.	Act on feedback. Reflect on outcomes. Use SOLO question prompts.

LI: Demonstrate knowledge of a concept

	Prestructural	Unistructural	Multistructural	Relational	Extended abstract
Demonstrate knowledge of a concept	I need help to demonstrate knowledge of a concept.	I can identify one relevant datum (or isolated data set).	I can identify several relevant discrete pieces of data or data sets ...	... and I can integrate the data to create a chain of logical reasoning tied to the concrete experience of the concept. I can relate findings to the concept ...	... and I can extend this to get an overview of abstract concepts. I can develop a proof. I can form a generalisation using correct mathematical statements.
Effective strategies [Insert strategies suggested by students and teachers]	Model. Show examples. Demonstrate. Give opportunity to practise. Reflect on outcomes. Use SOLO question prompts.	Give clear instructions. Prompt. Do situational teaching. Reflect on outcomes. Use SOLO question prompts.	Revisit, recap and remind. Reflect on outcomes. Use SOLO question prompts.	Give repeated opportunities to practise and reflect on outcomes. Use SOLO question prompts.	Act on feedback. Reflect on outcomes. Use SOLO question prompts.

LI: Use algorithms

	Prestructural	Unistructural	Multistructural	Relational	Extended abstract
Use algorithms.	I need help to start.	I can follow a one-step algorithm.	I can follow an algorithm that involves a number of steps …	… and I can check for errors and inconsistencies and reconstruct missing elements …	… and I can use this process as the beginning of a higher-level procedure.
Effective strategies [Insert strategies suggested by students and teachers]	Model. Show examples. Demonstrate. Give opportunity to practise. Reflect on outcomes. Use SOLO question prompts.	Give clear instructions. Prompt. Do situational teaching. Reflect on outcomes. Use SOLO question prompts.	Revisit, recap and remind. Reflect on outcomes. Use SOLO question prompts.	Give repeated opportunities to practise and reflect on outcomes. Use SOLO question prompts.	Act on feedback. Reflect on outcomes. Use SOLO question prompts.

LI: Identify values and trends from a graph, table or equation

	Prestructural	Unistructural	Multistructural	Relational	Extended abstract
Identify values and/or trends from a [graph, table or equation].	I need help to connect features from the [data display] with the context. Example: I reference personal experience to explain a feature.	I can read a value or a trend from a [data display].	I can read values or trends from the [data display], but I cannot explain them using the context presented.	I can read values or trends from the [data display]. I can explain what they mean in context …	… and I can question (evaluate) the reliability of the data or trend. I can suggest alternative meanings.
Effective strategies [Insert strategies suggested by students and teachers]	Model. Show examples. Demonstrate. Give opportunity to practise. Reflect on outcomes. Use SOLO question prompts.	Give clear instructions. Prompt. Do situational teaching. Reflect on outcomes. Use SOLO question prompts.	Revisit, recap and remind. Reflect on outcomes. Use SOLO question prompts.	Give repeated opportunities to practise and reflect on outcomes. Use SOLO question prompts.	Act on feedback. Reflect on outcomes. Use SOLO question prompts.

LI: Describe data presented in charts, graphs, tables or equations

	Prestructural	Unistructural	Multistructural	Relational	Extended abstract
Describe data in a data display – chart, graph, table or equation. (Reading within the data – charts, graphs, tables or equations)	I need help to describe data in a [insert data display].	I can identify features and units in a [insert data display].	I can identify features and units in a [insert data display].	… and I can explain what they mean in context and use them to identify trends. I can recognise the same data in different displays … Example: "has the same effect"	… and I can evaluate the advantages and limitations of different data displays in representing data and showing trends in context.
Effective strategies [insert strategies suggested by students and teachers]	Model. Show examples. Demonstrate. Give opportunity to practise. Reflect on outcomes. Use SOLO question prompts.	Give clear instructions. Prompt. Do situational teaching. Reflect on outcomes. Use SOLO question prompts.	Revisit, recap and remind. Reflect on outcomes. Use SOLO question prompts.	Give repeated opportunities to practise and reflect on outcomes. Use SOLO question prompts.	Act on feedback. Reflect on outcomes. Use SOLO question prompts.

LI: Organise data presented in charts, graphs, tables or equations

	Prestructural	Unistructural	Multistructural	Relational	Extended abstract
Organise data presented in a data display – chart, graph, table or equation.	I need help to group data in data displays.	I can organise one group of data in a data display.	I can organise groups of data in a data display …	… and I can explain why I have grouped the data using mathematical language … Example: Grouping data according to measures of centre – mean, median, mode, mid-range, outliers.	… and I can make a summary or generalisation based on the spread of the data in data displays.
Effective strategies [Insert strategies suggested by students and teachers]	Model. Show examples. Demonstrate. Give opportunity to practise. Reflect on outcomes. Use SOLO question prompts.	Give clear instructions. Prompt. Do situational teaching. Reflect on outcomes. Use SOLO question prompts.	Revisit, recap and remind. Reflect on outcomes. Use SOLO question prompts.	Give repeated opportunities to practise and reflect on outcomes. Use SOLO question prompts.	Act on feedback. Reflect on outcomes. Use SOLO question prompts.

LI: Represent data in charts, graphs, tables or equations

	Prestructural	Unistructural	Multistructural	Relational	Extended abstract
Represent data in a chart, graph, table or equation.	I need help to construct a [data display] for a given data set.	I can construct a [data display] for a given data set if I am instructed or directed.	I can construct a [data display] for a given data set but I cannot explain what it means in relation to the context presented.	I can construct a [data display] for a given data set and I can explain what it means in relation to the context …	… and I can construct alternative [data displays] for a given data display and use them to justify why one might be better at representing the data than another.
Effective strategies [Insert strategies suggested by students and teachers]	Model. Show examples. Demonstrate. Give opportunity to practise. Reflect on outcomes. Use SOLO question prompts.	Give clear instructions. Prompt. Do situational teaching. Reflect on outcomes. Use SOLO question prompts.	Revisit, recap and remind. Reflect on outcomes. Use SOLO question prompts.	Give repeated opportunities to practise and reflect on outcomes. Use SOLO question prompts.	Act on feedback. Reflect on outcomes. Use SOLO question prompts.

LI: Analyse data presented in charts, graphs, tables or equations – read between

	Prestructural	Unistructural	Multistructural	Relational	Extended abstract
Read between (compare) the data presented in charts, graphs, tables and/or equations.	I need help to compare (read between) the data presented in [data displays].	I can compare the data in [data displays] if I am instructed or directed.	I can compare the data in [data displays] and identify similarities and differences.	I can compare the data in [data displays] and I can explain why the data are similar and/or different …	… and I can use the similarities and differences to identify trends in the data and/or make inferences and predictions about the data.
Effective strategies [Insert strategies suggested by students and teachers]	Model. Show examples. Demonstrate. Give opportunity to practise. Reflect on outcomes. Use SOLO question prompts.	Give clear instructions. Prompt. Do situational teaching. Reflect on outcomes. Use SOLO question prompts.	Revisit, recap and remind. Reflect on outcomes. Use SOLO question prompts.	Give repeated opportunities to practise and reflect on outcomes. Use SOLO question prompts.	Act on feedback. Reflect on outcomes. Use SOLO question prompts.

LI: Interpret data presented in charts, graphs, tables or equations – read beyond

	Prestructural	Unistructural	Multistructural	Relational	Extended abstract
Read beyond (extend, infer, predict) the data presented in charts, graphs, tables and/or equations.	I need help to read beyond the data presented in [data displays].	I can read beyond the data presented in [data displays] if I am instructed or directed.	I can read beyond the data presented in [data displays] but I am not sure if my extension, inference or prediction is relevant.	I can read beyond the data presented in [data displays]. I can explain my extension, inference and/or prediction …	… and I can make generalisations about the reliability of the trends, inferences and predictions in the wider context. I can offer alternative explanations.
Effective strategies [Insert strategies suggested by students and teachers]	Model. Show examples. Demonstrate. Give opportunity to practise. Reflect on outcomes. Use SOLO question prompts.	Give clear instructions. Prompt. Do situational teaching. Reflect on outcomes. Use SOLO question prompts.	Revisit, recap and remind. Reflect on outcomes. Use SOLO question prompts.	Give repeated opportunities to practise and reflect on outcomes. Use SOLO question prompts.	Act on feedback. Reflect on outcomes. Use SOLO question prompts.

LI: Use function concepts in algebra to solve a problem

	Prestructural	Unistructural	Multistructural	Relational	Extended abstract
Use function concepts to solve a problem, using equations, graphs and tables.	I need help to use function concepts to solve a problem.	I can solve problems using one method of representation (eg, symbols).	I can solve problems using different methods of representation (eg, equation, graph or table). I see these as separate problems able to have different answers.	I can solve problems using different methods of representation. I make connections between different representations. I can use an answer to one representation to check the answers from other representations.	I can make connections between different representations and extend these ideas beyond the problem.
Effective strategies [Insert strategies suggested by students and teachers]	Model. Show examples. Demonstrate. Give opportunity to practise. Reflect on outcomes. Use SOLO question prompts.	Give clear instructions. Prompt. Do situational teaching. Reflect on outcomes. Use SOLO question prompts.	Revisit, recap and remind. Reflect on outcomes. Use SOLO question prompts.	Give repeated opportunities to practise and reflect on outcomes. Use SOLO question prompts.	Act on feedback. Reflect on outcomes. Use SOLO question prompts.

LI: Demonstrate a process to achieve an effect

	Prestructural	Unistructural	Multistructural	Relational	Extended abstract
Demonstrate a mathematical process to achieve an effect.	I need help to demonstrate a mathematical process. Example: Addition or subtraction	I can demonstrate a mathematical process. Example: Count all	I can use different mathematical processes to achieve an effect. Example: Count all, count both, count on, count on from larger, derived fact, known fact	I can explain why the different mathematical processes demonstrate the same effect. Example: Explain why they are all ways of carrying out the same process – addition	I can make generalisations about the most effective process used to achieve the effect (concept).
Effective strategies [Insert strategies suggested by students and teachers]	Model. Show examples. Demonstrate. Give opportunity to practise. Reflect on outcomes. Use SOLO question prompts.	Give clear instructions. Prompt. Do situational teaching. Reflect on outcomes. Use SOLO question prompts.	Revisit, recap and remind. Reflect on outcomes. Use SOLO question prompts.	Give repeated opportunities to practise and reflect on outcomes. Use SOLO question prompts.	Act on feedback. Reflect on outcomes. Use SOLO question prompts.

LI: Solve problems involving number sequences and patterns

	Prestructural	Unistructural	Multistructural	Relational	Extended abstract
Number sequences Patterns Technical vocabulary: ordinal language, pattern, sequence, repeat, same, different, continue addition, more than, less than, first, second, tenth etc, odd, even, multiples, predict, generalise, general term	I need help to investigate the number sequence or pattern.	I can describe a simple pattern/ relationship involving number sequences if directed (using diagrams, words, numbers, general terms).	I can describe a simple pattern/ relationship involving number sequences. But I am not sure about my method/ strategies and make mistakes.	I can describe a simple pattern/ relationship involving number sequences. I can make predictions about the number sequence and test them. I use this thinking to explain the relationships between terms in a number sequence …	… and I can make an algebraic expression and rule using a general term and mathematical notation to solve problems using a number sequence. I can apply the rule to solve the related situation.
Effective strategies [Insert strategies suggested by students and teachers]	Model. Show examples. Demonstrate. Give opportunity to practise. Reflect on outcomes. Use SOLO question prompts.	Give clear instructions. Prompt. Do situational teaching. Reflect on outcomes. Use SOLO question prompts.	Revisit, recap and remind. Reflect on outcomes. Use SOLO question prompts.	Give repeated opportunities to practise and reflect on outcomes. Use SOLO question prompts.	Act on feedback. Reflect on outcomes. Use SOLO question prompts.

LI: Apply numerical reasoning in solving problems (NCEA Level 1)

	Prestructural	Unistructural	Multistructural	Relational	Extended abstract
Numerical reasoning Ratio and proportion Factors, multiples, powers and roots Integer and fractional powers applied to numbers Fractions, decimals and percentages Rates Rounding with decimal places and significant figures Standard form	I need help to use [method].	I can use [method] to solve a problem if directed.	I can use [a range of methods] to solve a problem. I am not always sure why, when or where I should use the methods.	I can use [a range of methods] to solve a problem by selecting and carrying out a logical sequence of steps. I can relate my findings using appropriate mathematical statements. I know when and where I need to use [insert a range of methods] to solve a problem.	I can devise a strategy to investigate or solve a problem. I can identify relevant concepts in context, developing a chain of logical reasoning, or proof. I can form a generalisation. I can use correct mathematical statements, or communicate mathematical insight.
Effective strategies [Insert strategies suggested by students and teachers]	Model. Show examples. Demonstrate. Give opportunity to practise. Reflect on outcomes. Use SOLO question prompts.	Give clear instructions. Prompt. Do situational teaching. Reflect on outcomes. Use SOLO question prompts.	Revisit, recap and remind. Reflect on outcomes. Use SOLO question prompts.	Give repeated opportunities to practise and reflect on outcomes. Use SOLO question prompts.	Act on feedback. Reflect on outcomes. Use SOLO question prompts.

SOLO rubrics in geometry and measurement

LI: Measure the volume of a rectangular construction

	Prestructural	Unistructural	Multistructural	Relational	Extended abstract
Measure volume.	I need help to measure the volume of a rectangular construction. Example: Counts squares on surfaces (area)	I can measure the volume of a rectangular construction if I follow a procedure or direction. Example: Counts visible cubes on external surfaces and if prompted counts invisible cubes	I can measure the volume of a rectangular construction by counting visible and invisible cubes. Example: Adds or multiplies layers of cubes to get a total volume	I can measure the volume of a rectangular construction by multiplying the length, breadth and height dimensions of the rectangular construction. Example: Uses a formula $V = L \times B \times H$	I can make predictions/inferences about the impact of changes in one dimension on changes in other dimensions.
Effective strategies [Insert strategies suggested by students and teachers]	Model. Show examples. Demonstrate. Give opportunity to practise. Reflect on outcomes. Use SOLO question prompts.	Give clear instructions. Prompt. Do situational teaching. Reflect on outcomes. Use SOLO question prompts.	Revisit, recap and remind. Reflect on outcomes. Use SOLO question prompts.	Give repeated opportunities to practise and reflect on outcomes. Use SOLO question prompts.	Act on feedback. Reflect on outcomes. Use SOLO question prompts.

LI: Find the area of a shape

	Prestructural	Unistructural	Multistructural	Relational	Extended abstract
Find the area of shapes.	I need help to find the area of a shape.	I can use a strategy to find the area of a shape if I am directed. Example: I can find the area of a shape using a grid of squares (graph paper).	I can use several strategies to find the area of shapes. Example: I can find the area of irregular shapes using a grid of squares. I can find the area of regular shapes using formulas.	I can use several strategies in a logical order to find the area of a compound shape. I can explain the order … Example: I can find the area of compound shapes made up of regular shapes for which I know the formula.	… and I can use this thinking in new ways to find the area of complex compound shapes. Example: I can find the area of compound shapes made by adding whole and part regular shapes for which I know the formula.
Effective strategies [Insert strategies suggested by students and teachers]	Model. Show examples. Demonstrate. Give opportunity to practise. Reflect on outcomes. Use SOLO question prompts.	Give clear instructions. Prompt. Do situational teaching. Reflect on outcomes. Use SOLO question prompts.	Revisit, recap and remind. Reflect on outcomes. Use SOLO question prompts.	Give repeated opportunities to practise and reflect on outcomes. Use SOLO question prompts.	Act on feedback. Reflect on outcomes. Use SOLO question prompts.

LI: Identify shapes by their properties – angles

	Prestructural	Unistructural	Multistructural	Relational	Extended abstract
Identify angles.	I need help to identify clockwise and anticlockwise turns.	I can identify clockwise and anticlockwise turns and use these to identify a simple angle. Example: Right angle	I can identify and measure clockwise and anticlockwise turns and angles … Example: Right, acute, obtuse, straight, reflex angle; full turn – or 90, 180, 30, 45, 60	… and order, compare and explain the angles in different shapes.	… and I can use these relationships to estimate and predict angles in other contexts. Example: Angles around a point, vertically opposite angles.
Effective strategies [Insert strategies suggested by students and teachers]	Model. Show examples. Demonstrate. Give opportunity to practise. Reflect on outcomes. Use SOLO question prompts.	Give clear instructions. Prompt. Do situational teaching. Reflect on outcomes. Use SOLO question prompts.	Revisit, recap and remind. Reflect on outcomes. Use SOLO question prompts.	Give repeated opportunities to practise and reflect on outcomes. Use SOLO question prompts.	Act on feedback. Reflect on outcomes. Use SOLO question prompts.

LI: Identify shapes by their properties: two- and three-dimensional shapes

	Prestructural	Unistructural	Multistructural	Relational	Extended abstract
Identify 2D and 3D shapes.	I need help to identify common 2D and 3D shapes, triangles and quadrilaterals.	I can identify and describe the properties of common 2D and 3D shapes, triangles and quadrilaterals …	… and I can start to classify them on the basis of their properties …	… and I can explain why I have classified them … Example: By how many right angles, regular or not, symmetrical properties	… and I can use this to generalise about their properties, and/or make predictions about their symmetry.
Effective strategies [Insert strategies suggested by students and teachers]	Model. Show examples. Demonstrate. Give opportunity to practise. Reflect on outcomes. Use SOLO question prompts.	Give clear instructions. Prompt. Do situational teaching. Reflect on outcomes. Use SOLO question prompts.	Revisit, recap and remind. Reflect on outcomes. Use SOLO question prompts.	Give repeated opportunities to practise and reflect on outcomes. Use SOLO question prompts.	Act on feedback. Reflect on outcomes. Use SOLO question prompts.

LI: Operate with reflective symmetry tasks – line symmetry transformations

	Prestructural	Unistructural	Multistructural	Relational	Extended abstract
Perform line symmetry transformations on a series of points.	I need help to attack the task in an appropriate way.	I can reflect a point (coordinate) in a mirror line.	I can reflect various points in their respective lines of symmetry …	… and I can label the coordinates of the points correctly. I can justify the coordinate labels in terms of the reflection task …	… and I can make a generalisation about the effect of the transformation on any point in the cartesian plane. Example: I can make an algebraic formula describing the effect of the transformation.
Effective strategies [Insert strategies suggested by students and teachers]	Model. Show examples. Demonstrate. Give opportunity to practise. Reflect on outcomes. Use SOLO question prompts.	Give clear instructions. Prompt. Do situational teaching. Reflect on outcomes. Use SOLO question prompts.	Revisit, recap and remind. Reflect on outcomes. Use SOLO question prompts.	Give repeated opportunities to practise and reflect on outcomes. Use SOLO question prompts.	Act on feedback. Reflect on outcomes. Use SOLO question prompts.

LI: Operate with shapes – tessellation

	Prestructural	Unistructural	Multistructural	Relational	Extended abstract
Tessellate.	I need help to fit shapes together to tessellate (cover flat surface, no gaps or overlaps).	I can fit shapes together to tessellate.	I can fit shapes together to tessellate and identify common shapes that tessellate …	… and I can explain why shapes that tessellate fit around a point, using my knowledge of angles. I can explain why some shapes tessellate, using my knowledge of interior angles …	… and I can predict whether a shape can tessellate or not, using my knowledge of interior angles.
Effective strategies [Insert strategies suggested by students and teachers]	Model. Show examples. Demonstrate. Give opportunity to practise. Reflect on outcomes. Use SOLO question prompts.	Give clear instructions. Prompt. Do situational teaching. Reflect on outcomes. Use SOLO question prompts.	Revisit, recap and remind. Reflect on outcomes. Use SOLO question prompts.	Give repeated opportunities to practise and reflect on outcomes. Use SOLO question prompts.	Act on feedback. Reflect on outcomes. Use SOLO question prompts.

LI: Operate with shapes – determine position, direction and movement

	Prestructural	Unistructural	Multistructural	Relational	Extended abstract
Determine position, direction and movement of a shape.	I need help to use mathematical language to describe position.	I can describe position.	I can describe position using compass directions …	… and I can explain it by plotting coordinates in one quadrant or all four quadrants …	… and I can make generalisations about the effect of movement on position, eg, using vectors.
Effective strategies [Insert strategies suggested by students and teachers]	Model. Show examples. Demonstrate. Give opportunity to practise. Reflect on outcomes. Use SOLO question prompts.	Give clear instructions. Prompt. Do situational teaching. Reflect on outcomes. Use SOLO question prompts.	Revisit, recap and remind. Reflect on outcomes. Use SOLO question prompts.	Give repeated opportunities to practise and reflect on outcomes. Use SOLO question prompts.	Act on feedback. Reflect on outcomes. Use SOLO question prompts.

© Essential Resources Educational Publishers Ltd

LI: Operate with shapes – construction and drawing

	Prestructural	Unistructural	Multistructural	Relational	Extended abstract
Construct and draw an identified shape.	I need help to make/draw a shape.	I can make/draw a shape.	I can make/draw a shape and identify simple nets …	… and I can explain how nets can make a shape (eg, cube) …	… and I can create different nets to make the same shape (eg, cube).
Effective strategies [Insert strategies suggested by students and teachers]	Model. Show examples. Demonstrate. Give opportunity to practise. Reflect on outcomes. Use SOLO question prompts.	Give clear instructions. Prompt. Do situational teaching. Reflect on outcomes. Use SOLO question prompts.	Revisit, recap and remind. Reflect on outcomes. Use SOLO question prompts.	Give repeated opportunities to practise and reflect on outcomes. Use SOLO question prompts.	Act on feedback. Reflect on outcomes. Use SOLO question prompts.

SOLO rubrics in statistics

LI: Use data to test a hypothesis

	Prestructural	Unistructural	Multistructural	Relational	Extended abstract
Use data to test a hypothesis.	I need help to make sense of a set of data (list or table form).	I can follow instructions to find any mean, mode, median or range in a set of data (list or table form). I can plot a scatter graph from raw data.	I can find the mean, mode and median and select the most appropriate average measure. I can describe the distribution of data in a scatter graph	I can explain/justify why the mean, mode or median is the most appropriate average to use when interpreting the data. I can compare the distribution of data in scatter graphs and explain (draw inferences from) the data distribution.	I can select the most appropriate data to test a hypothesis by referring to its original context. I can make predictions from the distribution of the data in scatter graphs, test the predictions, and prove or disprove the hypothesis.
Effective strategies [Insert strategies suggested by students and teachers]	Model. Show examples. Demonstrate. Give opportunity to practise. Reflect on outcomes. Use SOLO question prompts.	Give clear instructions. Prompt. Do situational teaching. Reflect on outcomes. Use SOLO question prompts.	Revisit, recap and remind. Reflect on outcomes. Use SOLO question prompts.	Give repeated opportunities to practise and reflect on outcomes. Use SOLO question prompts.	Act on feedback. Reflect on outcomes. Use SOLO question prompts.

LI: Describe variables in a data set

	Prestructural	Unistructural	Multistructural	Relational	Extended abstract
Describe variables.	I need help to identify the variables in a data set.	I can identify the variables in a data set.	I can identify the variables in a data set and their units …	… and I can explain the variables by referring to an everyday context …	… and I can make predictions about the variables by referring to an everyday context.
Effective strategies [Insert strategies suggested by students and teachers]	Model. Show examples. Demonstrate. Give opportunity to practise. Reflect on outcomes. Use SOLO question prompts.	Give clear instructions. Prompt. Do situational teaching. Reflect on outcomes. Use SOLO question prompts.	Revisit, recap and remind. Reflect on outcomes. Use SOLO question prompts.	Give repeated opportunities to practise and reflect on outcomes. Use SOLO question prompts.	Act on feedback. Reflect on outcomes. Use SOLO question prompts.

LI: Organise data

	Prestructural	Unistructural	Multistructural	Relational	Extended abstract
Organise data.	I need help to organise the data in a meaningful way.	I can organise the data in a way/shape to show one aspect. Example: The shortest person is male.	I can organise the data in a way/shape to show several aspects. Example: The shortest person is male. The tallest person is male. Most of the females are 150-something.	I can organise the data in a way/shape to show several aspects and make links between relevant aspects of the data set … Example: Most of the females are 150-something and most of the males are between 150 and 170 cm. This indicates the heights of the females are more grouped together and the males are more spread.	… and I can make generalisations from my data. Example: Most of the females are 150-something and most of the males are between 150 and 170 cm. This suggests that proportionally males are taller than females. I can make predictions from my data. I can critically evaluate the usefulness of the way I have organised my data and suggest improvements.
Effective strategies [Insert strategies suggested by students and teachers]	Model. Show examples. Demonstrate. Give opportunity to practise. Reflect on outcomes. Use SOLO question prompts.	Give clear instructions. Prompt. Do situational teaching. Reflect on outcomes. Use SOLO question prompts.	Revisit, recap and remind. Reflect on outcomes. Use SOLO question prompts.	Give repeated opportunities to practise and reflect on outcomes. Use SOLO question prompts.	Act on feedback. Reflect on outcomes. Use SOLO question prompts.

LI: Compare and contrast different ways of organising data

	Prestructural	Unistructural	Multistructural	Relational	Extended abstract
Compare and contrast ways of organising data.	I need help to make comparisons between the two different ways of organising the data.	I can find one relevant way in which the organisation of data is similar and one relevant way in which it is different.	I can find several relevant ways in which the organisation of data is similar and several relevant ways in which it is different …	… and I can give reasons for the significant similarities or differences …	… and I can critically evaluate the relative merits for each way of organising data and give reasons and examples for any judgement made. I can predict other situations where these ways of organising data might be useful.
Effective strategies [Insert strategies suggested by students and teachers]	Model. Show examples. Demonstrate. Give opportunity to practise. Reflect on outcomes. Use SOLO question prompts.	Give clear instructions. Prompt. Do situational teaching. Reflect on outcomes. Use SOLO question prompts.	Revisit, recap and remind. Reflect on outcomes. Use SOLO question prompts.	Give repeated opportunities to practise and reflect on outcomes. Use SOLO question prompts.	Act on feedback. Reflect on outcomes. Use SOLO question prompts.

LI: Reflect on the statistical inquiry process (PPDAC)

Statistical inquiry process – PPDAC

SOLO level	Problem The statement of the research questions	Plan Planning the procedures used to carry out the study	Data The data collection process	Analysis The summaries and analyses of the data to answer the questions	Conclusion The conclusions about what has been learnt
Prestructural	No relevant focusing questions	• Little resource planning evident • Gantt chart research tasks and timeline incorrect or inconsistent	• Some information collected and recorded from limited resources • Recording unclear and/or inappropriate for the task	• Information simply represented without analysis • Only one data representation method	• Some attempt to sum up but no generalisation evident • No valid attempt at evaluation (in terms of evaluation of topic findings and/or reflection on the research process)
Unistructural	Some relevant focusing questions framed around simple factual recall (eg, who, what, why, when, where questions)	• Some resource planning evident • Gantt chart research tasks and timeline generally correct with some errors or omissions	• Some accurate and relevant information collected from more than one type of resource • Recorded clearly and appropriately	• Some information analysed appropriately (eg, evidence of definition, description, labelling, identifying) • More than one data representation method	• Some relevant ideas in a conclusion along with evidence of an attempt at generalisation • An attempt at evaluation of new understandings and the research process
Multistructural	Some relevant focusing questions framed around the research context	• Careful resource planning evident linked to the inquiry context • Gantt chart research tasks and timeline mostly correct and completed	• Clear, relevant and reliable information collected from different types of resource • Recorded clearly and appropriately in more than one format, method or platform	• A range of information analysed appropriately • A range of appropriate data representation methods used	• A range of relevant ideas in the conclusion and at least one reliable generalisation that includes evidence • A clear evaluation of the new understandings and the research process

continued ...

LI: Reflect on the statistical inquiry process (PPDAC) (continued)

Statistical inquiry process – PPDAC

SOLO level	Problem The statement of the research questions	Plan Planning the procedures used to carry out the study	Data The data collection process	Analysis The summaries and analyses of the data to answer the questions	Conclusion The conclusions about what has been learnt
Relational	Some relevant focusing questions framed around the research context (eg, define, describe, sequence, classify, compare, explain causes, analyse part–whole)	• Careful resource planning evident linked to the inquiry context • Gantt chart research tasks and timeline mostly correct and completed with an explanation provided	• Clear, relevant and reliable information collected from a range of relevant resources • Identification of quantities, variables, and units; explanation of variables by referring to the context • Recorded clearly and appropriately, including in more than one format, method or platform	• A range of information analysed appropriately (eg, evidence of definition, description, labelling, identifying and sequencing, classification, comparison, causal explanation, part–whole analysis) • A range of appropriate data representation methods used to make links between data	• A range of relevant ideas in the conclusion and at least one reliable generalisation that includes evidence • A clear and relevant evaluation of the new understandings and the research process
Extended abstract	An appropriate range of relevant focusing questions framed around the research context and beyond (eg, define, describe, sequence, classify, compare, explain causes, analyse part–whole, justify, generalise, predict, evaluate)	• Careful resource planning evident linked to the inquiry context and beyond • Gantt chart tasks and timeline all correct and completed with an explanation and prediction provided	• Collection of a wide range of clear, relevant, reliable and valid information from a diverse range of relevant resources • Choice of a range of clear, appropriate recording methods	• A wide range of information analysed appropriately (eg, evidence of [definition, description, labelling, identifying] and [sequencing, classification, comparison, causal explanation, part–whole analysis] and [evaluation, prediction, generalisation, creation]) • A wide range of appropriate data representation methods used to link, extrapolate and interpolate data	• Many relevant ideas in the conclusion, and valid generalisations given with evidence and/or predictions • A clear, relevant evaluation of the new understandings and the research process that includes personal reflection and prediction of where to next

© Essential Resources Educational Publishers Ltd

References and further reading

Biggs, JB. (2013). *Changing Universities: A memoir about academe in different places and times.* Australia: Strictly Literary.

Biggs, J and Collis, K. (1982). *Evaluating the Quality of Learning: The SOLO Taxonomy.* New York: Academic Press.

Biggs, J and Tang, C. (2007). *Teaching for Quality Learning at University: What the student does* (3rd ed). Berkshire: Society for Research into Higher Education & Open University Press.

Brosnan, P, Schmidlin, A and Grant MR. (2013). Successful mathematics achievement is attainable. In J Hattie and EM Anderman (eds) *International Guide to Student Achievement* (pp 348–350). New York: Routledge.

Chick, H. (1998). Cognition in the formal modes: research mathematics and the SOLO taxonomy. *Mathematics Education Research Journal*, 10(2), 4–26.

Davey, G and Pegg, J. (1989). Clarifying level descriptors for children's understanding of some basic 2-D geometric shapes. *Mathematics Education Research Journal*, No. 1, 16–27.

Ellington, AJ. (2013). The impact of calculators on student achievement in the K-12 mathematics classroom. In J Hattie and EM Anderman (eds), *International Handbook of Student Achievement* (pp 303–306). New York: Routledge.

Hattie, JAC. (2009). *Visible Learning: A synthesis of over 800 meta-analyses relating to achievement.* London: Routledge.

Hattie, JAC. (2012). *Visible Learning for Teachers: Maximising impact on learning.* London: Routledge.

Hiebert, J and Lefevre, P. (1986). Conceptual and procedural knowledge in mathematics: An introductory analysis. In J Hiebert (ed), *Conceptual and Procedural Knowledge: The case of mathematics* (pp 1–27). Hillsdale, NJ: Lawrence Erlbaum Associates.

Hook, P and Mills, J. (2011). *SOLO Taxonomy: A guide for schools. Book 1. A Common Language of Learning.* Invercargill: Essential Resources Educational Publishers Limited.

Hook, P and Mills, J. (2012). *SOLO Taxonomy: A guide for schools. Book 2. Planning for Differentiation.* Invercargill: Essential Resources Educational Publishers Limited.

Lake D (1999). Helping students to go SOLO: Teaching critical numeracy in the biological sciences. *Journal of Biological Education*, 33: 191–198.

McNeill, L and Hook, PJ. (2012). *SOLO Taxonomy and Making Meaning. Book 3.* Invercargill: Essential Resources Educational Publishers Limited.

Moritz, J and Watson, J. (1998). Longitudinal development of chance measurement. *Mathematics Education Research Journal*, 10(2), 103–127.

Pesek, D and Kirshner, D. (2000). Interference of instrumental instruction in subsequent relational learning. *Journal for Research in Mathematics Education*, 31, 524–540.

Skemp, R. (1976). Relational understanding and instrumental understanding. *Mathematics Teaching*, 77, 20–26,

Swan, MB. (2005). *Improving Learning In Mathematics: Challenges and Strategies.* UK: Department for Education and Skills.

Van Rossum EJ and Schenk SM (1984). The relationship between learning conception, study strategy and learning outcome. *British Journal of Educational Psychology*, 54: 73–83. doi: 10.1111/j.2044-8279.1984.tb00846.x

List of tables, figures, templates and rubrics

Tables

Table 1.1: Zooming in and out of fractions	6
Table 1.2: Self assessment rubric when working mathematically	7
Table 1.3: Question prompts to deepen students' mathematical thinking	8
Table 4.1: Numerical reasoning – writing the question assessment sheet	26
Table 5.1: Fractions question prompt rubric	41

Figures

Figure 1.1: SOLO symbols and hand signs	5
Figure 1.2: SOLO hand signs in use in a mathematics classroom	8
Figure 2.1: Student strategy for factorgram "Describe" problem	10
Figure 2.2: Student rubric for factorgram "Describe" problem	10
Figure 3.1: How can we represent number patterns?	14
Figure 3.2: Linear pattern (a) – Building a fence	14
Figure 3.3: Linear pattern (b) – Matchstick pattern	15
Figure 3.4: Linear pattern (c) – Taxi ride	15
Figure 3.5: Linear pattern (d) – Make up your own	16
Figure 3.6: Quadratic pattern (a) – Matchsticks	16
Figure 3.7: Quadratic pattern (b) – Handshakes	17
Figure 3.8: Year 9 student creates and makes links using like terms	18
Figure 3.9: Year 10 student's response to a class assessment	18
Figure 4.1: Describe + map for the King Arthur's College fundraising problem	23
Figure 4.2: Describe ++ map for Mike and Huia's exchange rate problem	25
Figure 4.3: Student responses to the fundraising problem using the Describe + map	27
Figure 4.4: Student responses to the exchange rate problem using the Describe ++ map	28
Figure 4.5: Student response to exam question	29
Figure 5.1: SOLO Hexagons for proper fractions	32
Figure 5.2: SOLO Hexagons for improper fractions	32
Figure 5.3: SOLO Hexagons for mixed fractions and picture fractions	33
Figure 5.4: SOLO Hexagons for algebraic fractions	33
Figure 5.5: SOLO Describe map for fraction groups	34
Figure 5.6: SOLO Compare and Contrast map for fraction groups	35
Figure 5.7: SOLO Describe map for measurement	36
Figure 5.8: Content for SOLO Hexagons activity on fractions, decimals and percentages	37
Figure 5.9: Sample method sheets for converting between fractions, decimals and percentages	38
Figure 5.10: End-of-unit fraction sum-up activity sheet	40
Figure 5.11: List of fractions for fraction sum-up activity	40
Figure 5.12: Assessment preparation diagram	41
Figure 5.13: Prior knowledge of fractions	42
Figure 5.14: Prior knowledge of measurement	43
Figure 5.15: Student response to SOLO Describe map for measurement	43

Templates

Template 2.1: Standard self assessment rubric for problem solving	11
Template 2.2: Simplified self assessment rubric for problem solving	12
Template 3.1: Self assessment rubric for representing number patterns	19
Template 4.1: HookED Describe + map	21
Template 4.2: HookED Describe ++ map	22
Template 4.1: Self assessment rubric for numerical reasoning	30
Template 5.1: Self assessment rubric for linking mathematical ideas	44

SOLO rubrics in number and algebra

Use appropriate methods/procedures to solve a problem	46
Demonstrate knowledge of a concept	46
Use algorithms	47
Identify values and trends from a graph, table or equation	47
Describe data presented in charts, graphs, tables or equations	47
Organise data presented in charts, graphs, tables or equations	48
Represent data in charts, graphs, tables or equations	48
Analyse data presented in charts, graphs, tables or equations – read between	48
Interpret data presented in charts, graphs, tables or equations – read beyond	49
Use function concepts in algebra to solve a problem	49
Demonstrate a process to achieve an effect	50
Solve problems involving number sequences and patterns	50
Apply numerical reasoning in solving problems (NCEA Level 1)	51

SOLO rubrics in geometry and measurement

Measure the volume of a rectangular construction	51
Find the area of a shape	52
Identify shapes by their properties – angles	52
Identify shapes by their properties: two- and three-dimensional shapes	52
Operate with reflective symmetry tasks – line symmetry transformations	53
Operate with shapes – tessellation	53
Operate with shapes – determine position, direction and movement	53
Operate with shapes – construction and drawing	54

SOLO rubrics in statistics

Use data to test a hypothesis	54
Describe variables in a data set	54
Organise data	55
Compare and contrast different ways of organising data	55
Reflect on the statistical inquiry process (PPDAC)	56

CPSIA information can be obtained
at www.ICGtesting.com
Printed in the USA
BVOW09s0242240117
474203BV00030B/127/P

9 781776 550067